MW00618591

The Closer

THE AUTOMOTIVE PROFESSIONAL'S
GUIDE TO CLOSING THE DEAL

Chris J. Martinez

J. JOSEPH GROUP

Copyright © 2023 by Chris J. Martinez.

Published by J. Joseph Group

All rights reserved. No part of this publication may be re-produced, distributed or transmitted in any form or by any means, including photocopying, recording, or other elec-tronic or mechanical methods, without the prior written permission of the publisher, except in the case of brief quo-tations embodied in critical reviews and certain other non-commercial uses permitted by copyright law.

The Closer / Chris J. Martinez. —1st ed.

ISBN 978-1-7355869-4-6 (paperback)
ISBN 978-1-7355869-5-3 (eBook)

Contents

To my dear wife, Veronica, who has always been my rock and my support system. Your unwavering love and belief in me have sustained me through the ups and downs of this writing journey. Thank you for always being there for me, and for being such an integral part of my life.

To my beautiful daughters, Jazmin, Janelle, Julianna, and to my son, Christian, who bring so much joy and light into my world. Your curiosity and enthusiasm for life inspire me every day, and I am grateful to have each and every one of you in my life. May you always be curious and open to new experiences, and may this book serve as a reminder of the limitless potential that lies within you all.

This book is dedicated to all of you, with love and gratitude.

INTRODUCTION

CLOSE: to bring (a business transaction) to a satisfactory conclusion.

I initially got into sales by chance. I didn't have a clear career path in mind and was looking for something that would challenge me and provide a good income. My twin brother suggested that I try working for CarMax, a company that sells used cars. I was hesitant at first, but I decided to give it a try.

Little did I know, I would end up staying in the car business for the next twenty years. I quickly found that I enjoyed the challenge of persuading people to buy a car and helping them find the right one for their needs. I also liked the fact that the pay was commission-based, so the harder I worked, the more money I could make.

People get into sales for many different reasons. Some people are drawn in because they enjoy the challenge of trying to persuade others to buy a product or service. Others may be attracted to the potential for high earnings and commission-based pay. Still others may be drawn to the opportunity to work with a wide variety of people and help them solve their problems. Ultimately, each of the reasons for pursuing a career in sales is as varied as the people who choose to do so.

As I continued to work in sales, I realized that the key to success was learning how to close deals. This took a lot of practice, a desire to find and follow the direction of good mentors, and a willingness to learn. It's often said that you can lead a horse to water, but you can't make it drink. My journey in the industry has included a lot of trial and error, but I was always willing to learn from the many great trainers and books available to me at any point in time.

Overall, I have found my career in sales to be incredibly rewarding. I've had the opportunity to help thousands of people find the right car for them, and I've been able to earn a great income while doing it. I've also had the opportunity to coach new and existing sales professionals as well as countless sales and finance managers in this industry. I wouldn't have it any other way.

With practice and the right attitude, anyone can become a master closer in the sales industry. This book highlights the tactical practices you can begin applying today in order to become one yourself.

CHAPTER 1

Let the Sale Begin

"THE SALE BEGINS WHEN THE CUSTOMER SAYS NO."
—Unknown

Let's start by clarifying the three types of sales professionals in the Automotive industry: the opener, the cooler, and the closer. Each of these individuals plays a different role in the sales process, and each is important in helping a business successfully sell its products or services. By understanding the different responsibilities each of these roles maintains, businesses can develop a sales strategy that is best tailored to their needs and the needs of their customers.

A sales opener is responsible for initiating contact with potential customers and introducing them to the product or service. This person might be focused on building a relationship with the customer and providing them with information about the product, rather than trying to persuade them to make a purchase. Depending on the context, a sales opener could also be indirectly involved in sales, as is the case with a customer service representative or a product designer. They are generally a new salesperson or someone who would typically fall in the order-taker category.

A sales cooler, on the other hand, is responsible for cooling down potential customers who are interested in making a purchase. This could involve providing them with more information about the product or service, answering any questions they might have, and addressing any concerns that might surface. The role of a sales cooler is often to help potential customers feel more comfortable and confident about their purchase and that they're making an informed decision. Depending on context, a sales cooler may also be involved in negotiating with potential customers to reach a mutually beneficial agreement. The cooler can close deals but is oftentimes afraid to ask tough questions to help push the customer over the edge toward making a purchase. The cooler is generally a more seasoned sales professional who performs well.

Finally, there's the sales closer. This is typically the person responsible for persuading potential customers to make a purchase. Because this can involve high-pressure tactics, negotiating, and other strategies designed to convince the customer to buy the product or service, some people may find this role intimidating. The idea of trying to persuade someone to make a purchase can feel uncomfortable, especially if someone doesn't want to be seen as pushy or aggressive.

The closer is often a highly regarded role because this person is responsible for completing the sale and persuading the customer to make the purchase (which is often considered to be the most important and challenging part of the sales process, given that it often requires a high level of skill, knowledge, and persuasion to convince the customer to buy). A successful closer can overcome objections, address any concerns the customer may have, and create a sense of urgency and desire for the product or service. They use a variety of tactics and techniques to persuade the customer and are able to adapt their approach to the individual customer and the specific situation. Because of the importance of this role, the closer is often rewarded with higher commissions or other incentives. This role in automotive can take years of practice, but those who are committed to learning and getting better every day can elevate themselves to great heights and master the art of closing.

That being said, there is a stigma often associated with being a closer, understandably referred to as "closer stigma." Stigma is the feeling of shame associated with a particular characteristic or trait that is considered to be socially unacceptable.

In any profession, a stigma can affect the way people perceive and interact with you. If your profession is in any way stigmatized, people may have negative or preconceived notions about you or your business, which can impact their willingness to engage with you or to take you seriously. That stigma can also affect the way you are treated by others, including potential clients. You may face discrimination or prejudice from others, which can make it more difficult for you to succeed in your field. By understanding whether your profession—or your role within your profession—has a stigma attached to it, you can be better prepared to address any negative attitudes or assumptions people may have and take steps to mitigate the impact of that stigma on your success.

There are a number of ways to mitigate the impact of stigma on your profession. One is, you can educate yourself about the stigma surrounding sales and understand the reasons why it may exist. This can help you to identify and challenge any negative assumptions or stereotypes people may have about salespeople. Additionally, you can be transparent and honest in your interactions with potential clients and avoid using high-pressure or manipulative tactics. This helps to build trust and credibility with clients and can show that you are a professional and ethical salesperson.

Examples of "High Pressure" or Manipulative Sales Tactics

FEAR OR ANXIETY
Using fear or anxiety to persuade the customer to make a purchase. This might involve making exaggerated or misleading claims about the potential consequences of not buying the product or implying that the customer is missing out on a limited-time offer or opportunity.

GUILT OR OBLIGATION
Using guilt or obligation to persuade the customer to make a purchase. One way people do this is by making the customer feel like they owe something to the salesperson, or that they are

being ungrateful or unappreciative if they don't buy the product.

FLATTERY OR INGRATIATION

Using flattery or ingratiation to persuade the customer to make a purchase. Perhaps the salesperson compliments the customer on their appearance, intelligence, or other qualities, or otherwise attempts to make them feel special or unique in order to persuade them to buy a product.

DECEPTION OR TRICKERY

Using deception or trickery to persuade the customer to make a purchase. Perhaps the salesperson hides important information about the product or its price or uses misleading or false claims to persuade the customer to buy the product.

AGGRESSIVE OR CONFRONTATIONAL TACTICS

Employing aggressive or confrontational tactics to persuade the customer to make a purchase. This can include the use of a loud or intimidating tone or making threats or ultimatums to pressure the customer into making a purchase.

Overall, these types of tactics are often considered unethical and unprofessional, and they can damage the trust and credibility of both the salesperson and the company. Instead of using these tactics, simply focus on building genuine, long-term relationships with customers as well as providing them with accurate and honest information about the product or service in order to persuade them to make a purchase.

There are many steps you can take to mitigate the impact of stigma on your sales profession. By being transparent, honest, and professional, and by building relationships and networks, you can help challenge the negative stereotypes and assumptions people may have about salespeople as you build a successful and fulfilling career in sales.

It's critical that you focus on building long-term relationships with clients, rather than just trying to make a quick sale. This demonstrates to customers that you are interested in meeting their needs and helping them solve their problems, not simply making a profit. Be prepared to address any objections or concerns that clients may have about working with you as a salesperson. This can help to overcome any negative attitudes or biases they may have about the sales profession while showing that you are knowledgeable and capable. Further, seek out opportunities to network and connect with other sales professionals, and share your experiences and insights when you do. This helps to build a supportive community of salespeople who can provide support, guidance, and mentorship, which can help to challenge any negative stigma associated with the profession.

CHAPTER 2

Why Closers Fail

There are many reasons why sales closers fail. Let's break them down so you have a better understanding of how they show up (and how you can avoid them).

LACK OF SKILLS OR KNOWLEDGE

"The only thing that separates successful people from the ones who aren't is the willingness to work very hard." - Helen Gurley Brown

One reason sales closers fail is that they don't have the necessary skills or knowledge to effectively persuade potential customers to make a purchase. Perhaps they have a lack of understanding of the product or service being sold or of the customer's primary needs and motivations. Or, maybe they lack effective communication and negotiation skills. Without these skills and this knowledge, a sale closer may struggle to convince potential customers to buy, even if that customer is extremely interested in the product or service.

"The art of persuasion is the art of making things easy, not difficult."
——*Benjamin Franklin*

TOO PUSHY OR AGGRESSIVE

Another challenge arises when a sales closer is too pushy or aggressive, which can turn potential customers off and make them less likely to buy. To be successful, closers must strike a balance between being persuasive and being respectful of the customer's wishes. If they are too pushy, they may come across as overbearing or insincere, which can quickly damage the relationship with the customer and make it less likely that they will make a purchase.

"Success is not final, failure is not fatal: it is the courage to continue that counts."
——*Winston Churchill*

INABILITY TO HANDLE OBJECTIONS

Some closers have an inability to handle objections or overcome obstacles that arise during the sales process. For example, a customer may have concerns about the price of the product, or they may have reservations about the quality or effectiveness of the product. If the closer is not able to adequately address these objections, they may struggle to convince the customer to make a purchase.

Closing a customer is obviously a crucial part of the sales process. It involves a series of steps that must be followed in order to successfully seal the deal. However, it is important to note that the closer (the individual responsible for closing the deal) may not always follow a structured process, and this lack of adherence to a proven process can lead to failure. Furthermore, it is important for the closer to be aware of their own emotional involvement and attachment to the deal, which can also negatively impact their ability to close it. In such cases, it may be beneficial to involve another manager or senior sales professional to take on the role of closing the deal, as they may be able to approach it with a more objective and detached perspective. This can be especially important when the closer is struggling with emotional intelligence and may be unable to effectively communicate and/or negotiate with the customer. Failing to identify where you are in the deal and not getting another manager or senior sales professional involved when it would be beneficial to do so can cause you to fail.

CHAPTER 3

Ethos, Pathos, and Logos

To persuade is, by definition, to provide sound reason for (someone) to do something.

Aristotle, a Greek philosopher and author who lived in the 4th century BC, first named and addressed ethos, pathos, and logos as rhetorical tactics in his book, *Rhetoric*. The study of rhetoric by Aristotle has had a lasting influence on communication and persuasion. As a result, the art and practice of persuasive communication with the intention of persuading and influencing people is referred to as rhetoric.

In *Rhetoric*, Aristotle outlined the three main modalities of persuasion—ethos, pathos, and logos—and how they might be utilized to persuade others. He maintained that in order to successfully persuade an audience, a speaker or writer must appeal to their reason, emotions, sense of trust, and credibility. Despite the fact that Aristotle's works on rhetoric date back more than 2,000 years, his theories on ethos, pathos, and logos are still extensively researched and used in a variety of industries, including sales.

The use of logic, emotion, and credibility to support and reinforce an argument are just a few of the many methods and tactics that can be employed to persuade an audience. When writing or speaking with the intention of persuasion and influence rather than merely providing information or facts, the term "rhetorical" is frequently employed. A sales pitch, for instance, can be said to be rhetorical because its goal is to persuade the listener to do something or believe something.

ETHOS

Ethos refers to the credibility and trustworthiness of the speaker or presenter. In sales, ethos can be established by highlighting the speaker's qualifications, expertise, and experience in the field. For example, a salesperson could mention their industry certifications, awards, or customer testimonials to establish their credibility and build trust with the customer.

PATHOS

Pathos refers to the emotional appeal of the argument or presentation. In sales, pathos can be used to create a sense of desire or urgency for the product or service being offered. This could involve using stories, images, or examples that evoke emotions and create a connection with the customer. For example, a salesperson could tell a compelling story about how the product has improved the lives of other customers or show pictures of happy customers using the product in order to create an emotional response and motivate the customer to make a purchase.

LOGOS

Logos refers to the logical and rational appeal of an argument or presentation. In sales, logos can be used to provide evidence and support for the product or service being offered. This could involve using statistics, data, or expert opinions to back up claims made about the product. In this case, a salesperson could provide information about the product's performance, safety, or efficiency to support their claims and help the customer make an informed decision.

As you become more practiced in using ethos, pathos, and logos in sales, you'll be able to create persuasive and compelling arguments that convince customers to make a purchase.

CHAPTER 4

How To Close A Deal

For a customer to agree to enter into a sales contract with you, they have to trust you. To establish trust with a customer, you must be confident and clear in your presentation of information. This means being an expert in the product or service you are offering and being able to provide detailed and technical information. The customer may have done their own research, so you must be prepared to answer any questions they have and provide certainty in your responses.

Trust is not something that is automatically given. Rather, it is earned by demonstrating expertise and a deep understanding of the product. To do this effectively, you must be able to identify the customer's true needs and be willing to recommend different options that may be better suited to their needs, even if those options differ from their original request. By doing so, you can open their mind to new possibilities and show that you truly understand their needs.

The only way they're going to trust you is if you build certainty. They must believe that you are a technical expert in your area. You must be the authority. You have to know your product—the specific vehicle you are trying to sell to the customer—inside and out as well as the financial terms you're trying to get the customer to agree to. The buck stops with you unless, in rare circumstances, you must get a manager involved. When a customer asks you a question, you must have more than enough product knowledge, because most customers have done their research prior to engaging with you. They will test you to verify that their information is correct, and if you aren't **certain** in your delivery of the information, you won't gain their trust.

Oren Klaff said it best: *"You must be able to speak at a pace and at a technical level... To show that you have done this thousands of times before and that there is no price negotiations. If you can say something at about twice the speaking rate in technical terms... that you could not possibly be making it up, to communicate that you've solved this customer problem, or similar problem. Hundreds of times before and you identify a problem*

CHAPTER 5

Know the Product You're Selling

Gaining a thorough understanding of the products and services offered by your dealership is an essential component of being a master closer in the automotive industry. Here are some steps you can take to ensure success in this area:

FAMILIARIZE YOURSELF WITH THE PRODUCT LINE

Take the time to learn about each product and service offered by your dealership or company. This includes understanding the features and benefits of each product as well as any financing or leasing options that may be available.

ATTEND TRAINING SESSIONS

Many automotive companies offer regular training sessions for their sales staff. These sessions can provide valuable information about new products and services as well as tips and techniques for selling them effectively.

CONDUCT RESEARCH

Stay up to date on industry trends and new products by conducting research online or attending industry conferences and events. This will help you to stay informed and able to provide accurate and relevant information to potential customers. I've personally closed deals with third-party information countless times. Using literature like Consumer Reports, Motor trends, and Automotive News can and will help you close more deals. Having the information readily available is key. Invest the money to have the magazines and news articles available.

ASK QUESTIONS

If you're unsure about something, don't be afraid to ask questions. Your manager or colleagues can be a great resource for information and guidance.

PRACTICE YOUR PRODUCT KNOWLEDGE

The more comfortable you are talking about your products and services, the more confident and persuasive you will be when selling them to customers. Consider practicing your product knowledge with colleagues or friends to gain confidence and improve your presentation skills. By taking these steps and continually seeking out opportunities to learn and improve, you can ensure that you have a thorough understanding of the products and services offered by your dealership or company.

Having a thorough understanding and knowledge of the product you are selling is essential for mastering the art of closing a deal. Without a deep understanding of the product, it is difficult to effectively communicate its value and benefits to potential customers, which can hinder your ability to close the sale. **It's not about only being able to recite product information but also having the ability to tailor your pitch to the specific needs and concerns of the customer**. This requires an in-depth understanding of the product's features and capabilities as well as its competitive landscape in the market.

Additionally, having knowledge of the product will help you to anticipate and address any objections or concerns that the customer may have, which can further increase the likelihood of closing the deal.

CHAPTER 6

Identify Objections

I t's important to know how to identify and properly flush out an objection. One approach is to actively listen to the customer and pay attention to any hesitations or concerns they express. Another is to ask open-ended questions that encourage the customer to provide more detailed feedback, such as "What concerns do you have about this product?" or "How does this compare to what you're currently driving?" Additionally, you can use reflective listening techniques, which means seeking to understand the customer, and offering the idea back to the customer to confirm the idea has been understood correctly as described previously. This can be done by repeating back the customer's objection in your own words in order to confirm that you understand their concern and can address it effectively. This technique is also known as mirroring, which we will breakdown later in the book.

By using these strategies, you can identify and address objections in a way that helps build trust and move the sale forward. Sometimes, you can cut to the chase and pull the objection right out of the customer. You do this by isolating the objection. One of my favorite techniques for doing this is, when a customer says, "I need to think about it" or "It's a big decision" (or any variation of that), the response should almost always be *"Okay, other than the fact that you need to think this through, is there any other reason you would not move forward?"* Give the customer the opportunity to speak up about exactly what will help them move forward. Once they've given you that answer, simply follow up with the following statement. *"So, what you're saying is that if I can do that, we can move forward?"* By doing this, you're throwing the ball back in their court to allow them to agree. When they do so, you immediately say, *"Perfect. I just need your initials here, and I'll get with my manager to see if I can get that done for you."* Turn the piece of paper around after pointing to where you need them to initial, and stay quiet. Asking for the commitment on everything you do is vital in order to move forward. Always get a commitment from the consumer. I've seen it happen countless times: a sales professional says a customer will move forward if we do thus-and-such, but it's not in writing. The minute they get it in writing, the deal changes and the customer ends up "craw fishing," or back peddling.

Once, when I was working on the showroom floor, I had a customer who wanted a specific truck with specific options. He told me that under no conditions would he buy a red truck. Red trucks reminded him of fire engines. Wouldn't you know it, the only vehicle I had with the specific features he wanted was red. I still showed it to him. I did a walk around and said, "It's everything that you said you wanted. Unfortunately, it's red, but on this truck, the red looks good!"

I couldn't sell him on it, so I said, *"Let's go to my office. I'll show you what the payments are going to be, and maybe we can order you one exactly like this in the color that you want."* (note: this small step is a huge difference maker that can turn an customer from a shopper to a buyer and we will talk more about the T-O later in the book) I took it to my manager, he gave me the numbers, and I tried again (twice) to close him on the deal. For me it ended as a no go. I tapped out and went to my closer. He went in on the turn, and within five minutes he came back out and said, "Wrap up your deal." What's even more amazing is, all he said to get the customer to say yes was, "Would you go color blind for one heck of a deal? I mean, a smoking deal?" The customer said yes. I don't recommend this if you are trying to hold your margin, but it works when you are absolutely at the last effort and your managers need to move a unit.

That taught me a valuable lesson about a close I didn't know of at the time. What the closer said was, "Sir, it's got the right options and features. It's just red. Would you be willing to be color-blind for a heck of a deal?" To that, the customer said yes. We discounted the price and put a car on the road.

Sometimes, the customer is more inclined to make a deal because it offers them value beyond a great price. That value could come in the form of additional features or benefits, a limited-time offer or discount, or a sense of exclusivity. For example, a customer may be more interested in a package deal that includes a free maintenance plan and extended warranty than they would be in a discounted price of the vehicle all by itself. By offering a deal that provides additional value, you can help create a sense of excitement and emotional involvement for the customer, which can make them more likely to make a purchase. Always ask for the sale, no matter what, but more importantly, if they're stuck on color, ask them if they'd be willing to be color-blind for a heck of a deal!

One of my closers years ago told me about a time he closed a deal based on pinstripes. I thought it was a funny story until I was faced with a similar situation. When you're selling an idea, it's important to be clear and concise when you explain the value and benefits of the idea to the customer. This can be done through effective communication and storytelling, using concrete examples and data to support your argument. Additionally, you can use persuasive techniques, such as highlighting the potential gains or addressing potential objections, to help convince the customer of the idea's value. It can also be helpful to create a sense of urgency or exclusivity, such as offering a limited-time discount or a special bonus for early adopters, to motivate the customer to act. By presenting a compelling and well-supported argument for your idea, you can increase your chances of convincing the customer to buy into it.

I once had a customer come in wanting a V6 Rav4 with all the options, which presented me with a big problem. We had only one V6, and it didn't have any options. However, she also wanted the car in light blue, and the V6 I had was white (with no options). I remembered what the closer had said to get the customer to purchase the red truck, so I tried it. I said, "Look, the good thing is that we can add leather to this vehicle, and it'll basically have the options you said you really want. Outside of that, I can put a blue pinstripe on it, which will put some contrast on it and make it look very appealing." Miraculously, she saw the vision I painted and wanted to move forward with the deal.

Sometimes, you have to paint a picture to entice your customer to want the vehicle you're trying to sell. Had I gone the direction most do, I would have been stuck trying to order the vehicle. The customer would have waited six months for the vehicle to arrive (if she didn't go to another dealer or brand due to being impatient). However, I took the approach of finding a way to sell her what I had in stock, and she fell in love with the vehicle—even preferring it white with the blue pinstripe! I have never seen anyone more excited about a vehicle than she was when she took delivery.

As sales professionals, we must remember that what we have in stock may not be exactly what the customer wants; we just need to show it to them in a different light. Remember, 80% of the time the customer ends up buying something different from what they originally came in to purchase. By showing the product or service in a different light and highlighting its unique features and benefits, you can help the customer see its value and potential for meeting their needs. This is especially important when the customer is unsure of what they want, or when they have specific requirements that may not be immediately apparent. By presenting the product or service in a new and compelling way, you can increase the chances of making a successful sale.

I once went on a turn for another sales professional, one who was a top salesperson in the store. All I did to close the deal was reclarify and reconfirm the numbers and ask him to move forward. He promptly agreed and signed the document. Reclarifying the deal is important, because it helps ensure that both the salesperson and the customer are on the same page and understand the terms of the agreement. This can help prevent misunderstandings as well as instances of miscommunication, which can lead to dissatisfaction or even disputes down the line. By taking the time to clearly and concisely explain the terms of the deal, the salesperson can help the customer understand exactly what they are getting and what they can expect. This builds trust and confidence in both the salesperson and the deal, which increases the likelihood of a successful sale. Sometimes, all it takes is a different face or a simple reclarification of the deal (and asking for the sale) to move forward. All too often, sales professionals simply cannot (or do not) ask for the sale. Do not get caught in this situation. *Always* ask for the sale.

As a closer, you must be willing to go all the way to finalize the deal. This means that you may have to occasionally take your client to lunch, go to their house (with management permission) to get their trade, or help them identify a cosigner. You may have to go so far as to do another walk-around on the vehicle as well as take them on another test drive. My sales professionals will confirm I have gone in on countless T-O's, however in my role today I'm not a huge fan of going in personally on deals, as much as I love doing so, because I know that, given how committed I get to closing a deal, it could end up taking two hours out of my day when I could instead be helping five to ten more sales professionals sell cars. I'm willing to go all the way (ethically) to close the deal, and sometimes that takes time!

CHAPTER 7

Practice Objections Handling

Handling and overcoming objections is an important skill for anyone in the automotive or any sales industry. Understanding common objections that customers may have and developing strategies for addressing them and persuading the customer to move forward with the deal is crucial for success in this field.

One of the first steps in handling objections is actively listening in order to fully understand the customer's concerns. Pay attention to what the customer is saying, ask clarifying questions if necessary, and acknowledge their concerns.

Common objections automotive customers have include concerns about price, financing options, and the reliability of the vehicle. It's important to address these objections directly and honestly, and to provide clear and concise responses. If a customer is concerned about the price of a vehicle, you might present information on the value or benefits of the vehicle or offer a variety of financing options. If a customer is concerned about the reliability of a vehicle, you might provide evidence of the vehicle's durability or reliability. Utilize third- party information from Consumer Reports, or Edmunds, and the like.

It's also important to remember that not all objections can be overcome. In these cases, it may be necessary to simply accept the objection and move on, which may involve offering alternative solutions or making a compromise.

Have you heard that it takes 10,000 hours to become an expert in your field? Sales trainer Andy Elliott talked about this idea during a meeting and shared his thoughts on three types of salespeople, asking which each of us wants to be:

Salesperson #1: Trains 1 hour a day for 365 days
Salesperson #2: Trains 1 hour once a week, or 52 times a year
Salesperson #3: Trains 1 hour a month, or 12 times a year

According to Elliott's analysis, it would take salesperson #2 seven years to catch up to salesperson #1, and salesperson #3 would need thirty years to catch up. In fact, it would take salesperson #1 twenty-seven years to become an expert, based on the 10,000-hour rule.

Some may argue that real-world experience can also be included in this training time. But the point remains that you should be training more than you might think. As Brad Lea once said, "Training isn't something you did, it's something you do."

So, how much *should* you be training? It's up to you to decide, but don't underestimate the value of consistent practice and learning.

Word tracks, also known as sales scripts, are important tools in sales because they provide a structure and guide for sales conversations. They help salespeople stay on track and ensure that they cover all the important points during a sales pitch.

Word tracks can be particularly helpful for salespeople who are new to the role, as they provide a framework for conversations and help a salesperson feel more confident and prepared. They can also be useful for experienced salespeople, as they can serve as a reminder of key points to cover as well as help keep the conversation focused.

In addition, word tracks can help salespeople identify any objections or concerns the customer may have and provide a framework for addressing those objections. This can help the salesperson build trust with the customer and ultimately close the sale.

Reaching mastery in the art of closing requires a consistent commitment to practice, rehearsal, and evolution of our craft. As we continue on this journey, let us remember the words of philosopher Lao Tzu: "The journey of a thousand miles begins with a single step." Let us embrace the challenge of learning and growing, and keep moving forward towards greater mastery and success.

"And don't be afraid to mess up."
—*Chuck Griffith*

CHAPTER 8

Understand The Power of The T-O

People often think that closing the deal means you must *personally* close a deal. What they don't understand is that if you want to close more deals, the strategy to employ is: If you can't close it, get someone else to help you close it.

A T-O (or turn-over) is when a salesperson recognizes that they are running out of **time or talent** to successfully close a deal with a customer. Rather than continuing to try and close the deal themselves, they bring in a manager or senior sales professional to take over the conversation and try to close the deal. This can be an effective strategy, because managers and senior sales professionals often have more experience and expertise in closing deals, and they may be able to provide additional value to the customer that the original salesperson was unable to.

I have always been a strong believer in the power of the T-O, and I recommend using it whenever you need to close a deal or overcome a challenge. When it feels like you're running out of time, the T-O can be a valuable tool for identifying where there might be bottlenecks or inefficiencies in your sales process. And later on, by analyzing the T-O, a business can identify which stages of the sales cycle are taking the longest, and where there might be opportunities to streamline or improve the process. This is especially important when a company is under time pressure, such as when it needs to meet a deadline or is facing a competitive threat.

I've closed more deals in my career because I realized when I ran out of time or talent. The best closers close more deals because they have better time management or bring in better talent to help them close the deal. Running out of time requires that you be able to predict when the customer is about to leave. I never had the false belief that the customer was going to come back. All too often, we believe that we've made a friend, or we think, "The customer really likes me; he's coming back." Do not get caught up in this scenario.

Most of us have been in a situation, personally or professionally, where we've been moved into the friend zone. When a salesperson has "gone into the friend zone" with a customer, they've failed to move the conversation forward and have instead become too familiar or friendly with the customer. "This is the moment" when you have to politely excuse yourself and get someone else involved.

The game is simple: You do not get paid if a customer leaves. Your goal, therefore, is to use all the tools at your disposal to close every deal in front of you. So, if you're unable to close a deal yourself, you should politely excuse yourself and bring in someone else who has the skills and experience to do so.

Awareness is key to understanding or predicting when a customer is about to leave. How do you identify this? You must look for clues. Customers generally will say things like, "I'm about to go to an appointment" or "I've got limited time." When this happens, excuse yourself and get someone else involved. How do you excuse yourself? It's very simple. Just say, "Mr. or Mrs. Customer, I just thought of something that's going to help save you time and money. Give me one second." Then, walk away. This will help you transition into getting an actual manager or senior sales professional to help you.

The T-O can also be a valuable tool when the sales professional has run out of talent. In this scenario, the T-O can help the closer identify areas where it might be struggling to close deals. By analyzing the T-O, the closer can identify where it might need to invest in additional training or resources to support its sales team, or where it might need to consider hiring additional staff.

In either of these scenarios, it is important to involve a closer, manager, or senior sales staff member in the process of analyzing the T-O. This can help ensure that any recommendations or actions taken because of the analysis are well-informed and well-supported. A manager or senior sales staff member can provide valuable insights and expertise that can help a business make the most of the T-O as a tool for improving its sales performance.

I remember the day I learned the true power of the T-O. I was running a sales team and had a senior salesperson who was struggling to close a deal with a customer. He had tried everything he could think of, but the customer just wasn't interested.

At the time, I had a rule that I wouldn't get involved in the T-O. I knew it could be time-consuming, and when I get involved in deals, I stay all the way. If I need to re-demo the vehicle or take the customer home to get the trade, I will do that to ensure that the deal is closed. I always want to make sure I am available to support our other salespeople. In this case, I felt like I needed to step in, because everything the salesperson told me didn't add up. The deal sounded relatively easy to close. I told the senior salesperson to go back to the customer and explain that we could get them a lower rate if they stayed with us. I thought it was a straightforward pitch that would be easy to close.

To my surprise, the senior salesperson came back and told me that the customer still wasn't interested. I was starting to get frustrated, so I turned to one of my newer salespeople, who had only been with the company for a few weeks. I told her that if the senior salesperson couldn't close the deal, I would turn the customer over to her and let her try.

To my surprise, the senior salesperson was opposed to this idea. He told me that there was no way the customer would buy, no matter who tried to sell them. Starting to lose my patience even more, I told him that I was going to give the newer salesperson a chance to close the deal.

Within a few minutes, the newer salesperson had done just that. The senior salesperson was, of course, shocked and upset, but I was thrilled to see the power of the T-O in action. Sometimes, all it takes is a different face saying the same thing or clarifying the deal in a different way. It was an important lesson for not only the senior salesperson but our newer salesperson as well.

CHAPTER 9

7 STEPS OF THE T-O

There are seven critical steps of the T-O that are important to know and practice.

BE SEATED

It's important to be seated when you're talking to a customer about their objections. This helps you maintain control of the conversation, and it creates a more relaxed and comfortable environment. By inviting the customer to sit down in your office, you can create a sense of trust and establish a professional and respectful tone for the conversation.

BUILD TRUST

Building trust is crucial in any sales situation, and it is especially important when dealing with customer objections. One way to build trust is to let the customer know that you are committed to treating them fairly and addressing any concerns they may have. By demonstrating your commitment to their interests, you can create a sense of trust and establish a foundation for resolving the objection. A great example of a trust-building statement is: "I want you to feel like you're being treated fairly. So, please stop me if you feel like I'm being unfair at any time so we can address it."

BE THE AUTHORITY - CLARIFY THE DEAL

As a sales professional, it is important to establish yourself as the authority on the product or service you are selling. This means being knowledgeable and informative and being able to clearly explain the benefits and value of the product. By clarifying the deal and reiterating the terms, you can help the customer understand what they are agreeing to and reduce the likelihood of objections arising.

Don't give your customer a false sense of hope. You'll be surprised by the power of NO. Simply telling the customer NO is oftentimes enough to encourage them to simply move on. Always re-iterate the deal both you and the customer have come to. Simply by reaffirming the deal, you may be able to close the customer. Sometimes, saying it one more time for the customer is all you need.

QUESTION

Asking the right questions can be an effective way to draw out any underlying objections that a customer may have. Ask 'How' and 'What' questions to draw out any underlining objections.

For example: "We unfortunately cannot agree to your terms. What else can we do to help move this deal forward? How can we get to that number knowing what the market values are today?"

MIRROR YOUR CUSTOMER

Mirroring your customer involves repeating what they have said in an inquisitive way, to encourage them to elaborate on their objections and provide more information. This can be an effective way to understand their perspective and identify the underlying reasons for their objection. When mirroring, it is important to use a low and slow tone, and to pause after repeating their statement. This will show that you are listening and interested in their perspective and can help to create a sense of trust and understanding.

When you don't like the answer, the customer has given you, simply repeat the answer the customer said in an inquisitive way.

Example:

Customer: "I think your price is too high."
Negotiator: "My price is too high?"

Be sure to watch the way you say it. Again, your tone should be low and slow, and you should pause when you're finished repeating their statement. You may have to do this several times over the course of a negotiation.

GET THEM TO "THAT'S RIGHT!"

This is how you get to the aha moment. Once you and your customer are on the same page, you can use specific questions to help them return to the emotional reasons why they selected the vehicle in the first place. This can help to refocus their attention on the benefits and value of the product and encourage them to reconsider their objection.

Asking specific questions to get them back to the *emotion* of why they selected the vehicle in the first place gets them back in the right mindset.

For example: "How did you come to select this vehicle?" or "What made you pick this vehicle?"

ASK FOR THE SALE

You want to ask for the sale by using a closing technique that is tailored to the specific situation and the customer's needs. By turning to your arsenal of closes, you can effectively persuade the customer to make a purchase.

For example: "Doesn't it make sense to move forward then?" All we need is your signature and date, and we'll get your vehicle cleaned and ready for delivery." (At this point, you hand them a pen to sign the write-up.)

CHAPTER 10

Rules of Negotiation

There are many rules or principles that guide successful negotiations. In my experience, some of the most important include:

BE PREPARED

Before entering into a negotiation, it is important to do your research and gather as much information as possible about the other party, the issue at hand, and the potential outcomes of the negotiation. This will help you to identify your goals and priorities as well as develop a strategy for achieving them.

COMMUNICATE OPENLY AND HONESTLY

To reach a successful outcome, it is important to communicate openly and honestly with the other party. This means being clear and direct about your needs and interests *and* being willing to listen to and understand the other party's perspective. By creating an open and honest dialogue, you can build trust and establish a foundation for finding a mutually beneficial solution.

BE FLEXIBLE AND OPEN TO COMPROMISE

Negotiations often involve give and take, and it is important to be flexible and open to compromise in order to reach a successful outcome. This means being willing not only to listen to the other party's needs and interests but also to consider different options and solutions. By being open to compromise, you can find solutions that meet the needs of both parties and move the negotiation forward.

BE ASSERTIVE, BUT NOT AGGRESSIVE

It is important to be assertive in a negotiation, which means standing up for your own needs and interests. However, it is equally important that you avoid being aggressive or intimidating, as this can create tension and make it difficult to reach a successful outcome. By being assertive and respectful, you can effectively communicate your needs and interests, and create an environment in which both parties can reach a mutually beneficial agreement.

Before you enter into negotiations, you must understand your customer's goal. **Build a relationship with your customer**, and you're more likely to close the deal. At the end of the day, what you want is repeat customers, and being likable is an important aspect of effectively communicating and interacting with others, especially in a sales or customer service context. The saying "You get more flies with honey than with vinegar" came about precisely it is generally more effective to be friendly and approachable, not rude or confrontational. In his book, How to Win Friends and Influence People," Dale Carnegie, outlines several steps that can help you become more likable quickly, and I highly recommend that you grab a copy and take notes!

In short, be genuinely interested in your customer. Intently listen to them and ask good questions as opposed to simply talking about yourself or your product.

Wondering about some good questions to ask to get the conversation going? No problem! Here are some starting points:

- Have you had a chance to consider your budget or financing options?
- Are there any specific features or technologies that you're interested in that we haven't shown you?

- Have you had a chance to test drive any vehicles or do some research?

Asking questions can help you better understand the customer's needs and preferences and can also help to identify any potential challenges or objections you may need to address. By showing genuine interest in the customer's needs and actively listening to their responses, you can build trust and establish a more positive and effective interaction.

Always use the customer's name when speaking with them. Repeating their name during the interaction helps to make them feel more comfortable and connected to you. (It also helps you remember their name.!)

Smile, and smile often. Smiling is a simple but powerful way to create a more positive and friendly atmosphere. It can help to put the customer at ease and make them more open to what you have to say.

Be complimentary. Complimenting the customer three to four times during the transaction can help to make them feel valued and appreciated. It's important, however, to avoid overdoing it, as too many compliments can quickly begin to seem insincere.

CHAPTER 11

Sell The Deal, Not Just the Vehicle

n a recent study by Lending Tree, it was found that one in four people make a purchase decision based on a special deal or rate. This highlights the importance of promoting deals and discounts when making a sales pitch.

While some customers may be primarily focused on the product itself, others are more interested in the savings they can get by taking advantage of a special offer. In these cases, stressing the importance of the deal or discount can be a powerful motivator for the buyer.

For example, if a customer is considering purchasing a new car, highlighting the low interest rate or special financing options available can make the deal more appealing. In addition, emphasizing the limited-time nature of the offer can create a sense of urgency and encourage the customer to decide sooner rather than later. There was a time when Toyota was offering 0% financing to customers who had a credit score of 660 or better. This was a phenomenal deal. When I would talk to customers before they were leaving, I would tell them about how amazing this deal was, and it immediately piqued their interest. When a customer told me they didn't have the best credit, I would tell them about this opportunity, and it helped motivate them to try to buy that day. I remember selling more Corollas that month than any other salesperson at that store. It felt surreal. I couldn't believe people would buy the deal more than the vehicle. It was an *aha* moment, for sure.

It's important to remember that not all customers will be motivated by deals and discounts, and it's critical to tailor your sales pitch to each individual customer. However, for those who are interested in saving money, highlighting special offers can be a powerful tool to close the sale.

As a car salesperson, I have found that many customers are motivated to make a purchase decision based on the value they see in the lease payment, financing options, and other discounts and incentives. In these cases, it's important to focus on selling the deal by highlighting the benefits of taking advantage of these offers.

For example, when a customer is considering leasing a car, I make sure to stress the low monthly payment and the flexibility of a lease compared to financing a car purchase. I also highlight any special deals or incentives that are available, such as 0% financing or a cash back offer.

In addition, I emphasize the limited-time nature of these offers, which can create a sense of urgency. This can be especially effective when the customer is on the fence about making a purchase.

I have found that focusing on the deal as well as the value of the offers available is a powerful tool for closing sales. By selling the deal, not just the vehicle, I can convince more customers to make a purchase, which ultimately helps me to be more successful in my job as a car salesperson.

CHAPTER 12

Effective Closing Techniques

There are several closing techniques that can be effective in persuading a potential customer to make a purchase. Common closing techniques include:

THE ASSUMPTIVE CLOSE

This technique is used when it's assumed that the customer is ready to make a purchase, and the salesperson asks them to decide about specific details of the sale. For example, you might say something like, "Great, so which color would you prefer? Red or silver?" Or ask, "Can you confirm your delivery address?" while providing the customer with paperwork to sign.

This technique is often effective in creating a

sense of momentum and pushing the customer towards a decision. It can also be a subtle way of testing the customer's level of interest or commitment. However, if used too aggressively or without having first built sufficient rapport, the assumptive close can come across as pushy or presumptuous, which may turn the customer off.

THE "BECAUSE" CLOSE

This technique involves explaining the benefits of the vehicle or the dealership's services in order to persuade the customer to make a purchase. For example, you might say something like, "Our dealership offers a great financing program, because we work with a variety of lenders to get you the best rate possible." Or, you might further explain the features of a particular vehicle, the benefits of a particular financing program, or some lesser-known benefits of purchasing from your dealership.

This technique is effective in building trust and credibility because it demonstrates a thorough understanding of the product or service you are selling. It can also help to address any objections or concerns the customer may have. If, however, the rationale or benefits you present are not relevant or convincing, this technique may prove less than effective.

THE "FEAR OF LOSS" CLOSE

The "fear of loss" close involves creating a sense of urgency or scarcity to persuade the customer to make a decision, which can be particularly useful in situations where the customer is on the fence about making a purchase.

For example, "I have another customer interested in this vehicle, so if you'd like to make a purchase I recommend doing so soon."

Beyond mentioning that another customer is interested in the same vehicle, you can offer a limited-time discount or promotion or note that a particular model or option is in high demand and may not be available for much longer. If used too aggressively, however, or without having built sufficient rapport with the customer, the fear of loss close can come across as manipulative or pushy, which may have the opposite effect of what you're looking for.

THE "TAKE AWAY" CLOSE

This particular close involves presenting the customer with a choice between two options, and then taking away one of the options to create a sense of scarcity. For example, you might say something to the effect of "We have two financing options available: a 3-year loan or a 5-year loan. The 3-year loan has a slightly lower rate, but it's only available today. Which option would you prefer?" You can also utilize this type of close when you can offer two vehicle models to the customer, one of which is in limited supply.

Similar to the other closing tactics, if used too aggressively or without having created a comfortable relationship with the customer, this close may come across as manipulative, so be sure to give thoughtful consideration to when and how you use it.

It is important to use any of these techniques with caution and in a way that is ethical and respectful of the customer's needs and concerns. It is also important to be prepared to handle any objections your customer might raise and address any concerns the customer may have.

THE "PUPPY DOG" CLOSE

The "puppy dog" close is a successful closing strategy. It entails giving a prospective customer a chance to try out a good or service before deciding whether or not to buy. This allows the customer to use the product and see how it might alleviate the problem they're experiencing.

This method is named after the way puppies are often sold at pet stores. Prospective purchasers can engage and play with the puppies before making a purchase. Salespeople reduce the pressure of a purchase on the consumer while fostering a relationship of trust through this approach, which may result in a successful closing and a happy client.

It's important to utilize the "puppy dog" close regularly, as it can help to boost the success rate of closing agreements.

THE EMPATHIZE-JUSTIFY CLOSE

This approach entails acknowledging and empathizing with the client's worries, validating their viewpoint, and finally, offering a convincing justification for the problem at hand. The final step of the process is to provide or identify a solution that meets the needs of the customer. It's essential to listen intently; show empathy; and speak in a cool, collected, and professional manner in order to use this strategy successfully. This technique is useful for settling disputes and coming to an amicable conclusion in any sales situation when you're looking to overcome complaints or objections.

CHAPTER 13

The Importance of Language as a Closer

As an authority in the automotive sales industry, it is important for us to establish trust and credibility with our potential customers, which may include other dealerships. By using language that showcases our expertise and knowledge in the field, we can differentiate ourselves from competitors and make our business more appealing. Utilizing our extensive network of contacts, collaborating with our team, and implementing unique sales strategies, we can help become better at strategizing and reaching our goals for selling vehicles. Additionally, extensive knowledge of our product lines and a streamlined sales process can enhance our experience and increase our chances of success.

Some words that help enhance others' trust in our expertise and ability to steer them in the right direction include:

- Utilize
- Collaborate
- Maximize
- Strategize
- Implement
- Innovate
- Enhance
- Streamline
- Leverage
- Synergize

Sample sentences using these words that can help you sound like a pro

- We can utilize our extensive network of contacts to help you find the perfect vehicle.
- By collaborating with our team, you can maximize your chances of getting a great deal on the perfect vehicle for you.
- At our company, we use a unique sales strategy to help you strategize and reach your goals for selling your vehicle. Let's implement a plan to target potential

customers and increase the potential sale of your vehicle. (This works for dealers who consign vehicles)

- Our innovative product line is sure to enhance your business and set you apart from the competition.
- We can streamline the car sales process for you, making it faster and easier to achieve your goals.
- Leverage our team's expertise to improve your chances of getting you approved.
- By working together, we can create a synergy that will help you achieve your goals on your next purchase.

Using more sophisticated financial terms will also help build your credibility and a customer's confidence in you as the authority. Here are some basic terms and ways you can use them:

- The car you're interested in is an asset that will retain its value over time.
- If you have cash on hand, you can avoid the need for financing and get a great deal on your car.
- Our balance sheet shows that we have the financial stability to offer you a loan with a low interest rate.

- Our cash flow is strong, so we can offer you flexible payment options.
- The depreciation of your current car can be used as a trade-in to lower the price of your new vehicle.
- Your equity in your current car can be used as a down payment to help you buy your next one.
- If you have negative equity in your current car, we can help you find a loan with a low loan-to-value ratio.
- Our dealership has a low liability for loans, so we can offer you a great interest rate on your car loan.
- We can provide a free valuation of your trade-in, so you know exactly how much it's worth.
- Our dealership has a low profit margin, so we can offer you a great price on your car.
- If you have a high credit score, you may be eligible for a loan with a low interest rate and a high loan-to-value ratio.
- If you take out a loan to buy your car, we will place a lien on the vehicle until the loan is paid off.
- Your credit limit will determine how much you can borrow to buy your car.

- If you need to borrow money to buy your car, you may be asked to provide a personal guarantee.
- An appraisal will be performed on your trade-in to determine its value.
- Our income statement shows that we are a financially stable dealership with a strong track record of sales.
- There may be some stipulations in the loan agreement that you need to be aware of before signing.
- If you lease a car, the residual value is the estimated value of the car at the end of the lease.
- The money factor is a number that is used to calculate the interest on a car lease.
- Your FICO score will play a role in determining the interest rate on your car loan.
- Our dealership's EIN (Employer Identification Number) is 123-45-6789.

Using word tracks and knowing the terms will help you build your authority while helping to build your customer's confidence in you. Without credibility, the customer won't trust you or your dealership, which will make it difficult for you to close your deal.

CHAPTER 14

Understanding Buyer Personalities

The ability to identify a buyer's personality type is an important quality in a sales closer. It helps them tailor their approach and messaging to each individual customer. Different personalities will respond to different tactics and techniques, and by understanding each customer's unique personality, the closer can adapt their approach to better suit their needs and preferences.

For example, a customer with a more analytical personality may respond well to detailed information and logical arguments, while a customer with a more emotional personality may be swayed by stories and emotional appeals. By being attuned to the customer's personality, the closer can create a personalized and effective sales pitch that is more likely to persuade the customer to make a purchase.

There are many different types of personalities that a closer may encounter, and it can be helpful for them to be familiar with a number of them in order to be able to quickly adapt their approach and messaging accordingly.

COMMON PERSONALITY TYPES A CLOSER ENCOUNTERS

ANALYTICAL PERSONALITY

An analytical personality tends to be logical, rational, and detail-oriented. These individuals respond well to data, facts, and statistics, and may be more likely to make a decision based on a thorough analysis of the information provided.

EMOTIONAL PERSONALITY

An emotional personality tends to be more intuitive, empathetic, and sensitive. These individuals may be more influenced by stories, examples, and emotional appeals, and may be more likely to make decisions based on their feelings and values.

AMBITIOUS PERSONALITY

An ambitious personality tends to be driven, competitive, and focused on achieving goals. These individuals are typically more motivated by opportunities for growth, advancement, and success, and more likely to make decisions based on the potential benefits and rewards of the product or service.

SPONTANEOUS PERSONALITY

A spontaneous personality tends to be flexible, adaptable, and impulsive. These individuals may be more open to new ideas and experiences, and they're more likely to make a decision based on their current mood and impulses.

When it comes to quickly ascertaining a customer's personality type, I've always used the DECS method, which stands for Dominant/Driver, Ego/Expressive, Complacent/Amiable, Stable/Analytical.

DOMINANT/DRIVER PERSONALITY

A dominant/driver personality is characterized by a high level of ambition, competitiveness, and drive. These individuals tend to be focused on achieving their goals and may be motivated by opportunities for growth, advancement, and success. They are often assertive, decisive, and confident, and may be able to influence others and persuade them to follow their lead.

In a sales situation, a dominant driver personality may be more likely to make a quick decision and be open to new ideas and opportunities. A salesperson can best appeal to this personality type by highlighting the potential benefits and rewards of the product or service and presenting a compelling and confident argument for why the customer should make a purchase. You must be assertive and on task when working with a dominant/driver personality in order to be successful.

EGO/EXPRESSIVE PERSONALITY

An ego/expressive personality is characterized by a strong sense of self and a desire for attention and recognition. These individuals tend to be confident, outgoing, and extroverted, and often more focused on personal achievement and success than on teamwork or collaboration. You can usually identify them when they drive in and they usually have flashy clothes or a personalized license plate. They're more likely to express their thoughts and feelings openly and are often less concerned with the opinions and feelings of others.

In a sales situation, an ego/expressive personality may be more likely to be open to new ideas and opportunities and may be more influenced by personal gain and recognition than by the potential benefits to others. A salesperson can best appeal to this personality type by highlighting the potential personal rewards and recognition that the customer could gain from making a purchase and by presenting a confident and assertive argument for the product or service. Because they are ego-driven, it doesn't hurt to compliment them as much as possible!

COMPLACENT/AMIABLE PERSONALITY

A complacent/amiable personality is characterized by a low level of ambition, assertiveness, and drive. These individuals tend to be more focused on maintaining harmony and avoiding conflict than on achieving goals or success. They may be more inclined to follow the lead of others and less likely to take risks or make decisions on their own.

In a sales situation, a complacent/amiable personality may be more hesitant and unsure about making a purchase. They may need more information and reassurance before making a decision. A salesperson can appeal to this personality type by providing detailed and thorough information about the product or service and addressing any concerns or objections the customer may have. They may also be able to create a sense of comfort and security by offering guarantees, warranties, or other assurances that can help the customer feel more confident in their decision.

Customers with a complacent/amiable personality type are my favorite, as they are looking to connect with you on a personal level and generally desire a long-term relationship with their service providers.

STABLE/ANALYTICAL PERSONALITY

A stable/analytical personality is characterized by a high level of rationality, logic, and attention to detail. These individuals tend to be more focused on facts, data, and evidence than on emotions or personal experiences. They may be more inclined to make decisions based on a thorough analysis of the information available and less influenced by personal opinions or biases.

In a sales situation, a stable/analytical personality is more likely to be skeptical and critical of the salesperson's argument and may need a well-supported and logical presentation in order to be convinced to make a purchase. A salesperson can appeal to this personality type by providing detailed information about the product or service and by using data, statistics, and expert opinions to support their claims. They may also be able to overcome objections and address concerns by providing logical and well-reasoned responses.

Be prepared to have third-party data to back up most (if not all) claims you make. The higher the number of hard facts and data you provide, the easier it will be to close this customer. (I generally like to have a copy of Consumer Reports or Car and Driver handy when working with a customer who had this personality type).

CHAPTER 15

The Importance of Follow-Up

The process of buying a car is a significant and often time-consuming decision for consumers. According to a 2019 study conducted by Cox Automotive, the average consumer spends 96 days in the market before making a purchase. This highlights the importance of follow-up in the car sales process, as even if a salesperson is unable to close the deal on the first interaction with a customer, staying in touch can increase the chances of making a sale.

The follow-up is an essential element of the sales process that should not be overlooked. While it may be disappointing not to close a deal on the first interaction with a customer, it is important to remember that there are still opportunities to follow up and potentially close the sale at a later date.

One of the key benefits of the follow-up close is the ability to check in with the customer and see if there have been any changes in their needs or circumstances that may make them more receptive to the product or service being offered. By following up, you can also take the opportunity to reiterate the benefits of the product or service and address any new concerns or objections the customer may have.

There are several ways to follow up with a customer, including calling them, texting them, and emailing them. Each of these methods has its own advantages, and it is important to consider which approach is most appropriate for each customer and situation. For example, a phone call allows for more personal interaction and the opportunity to address any concerns or objections the customer may have, while a text or email can be a quick and convenient way to touch base.

Another effective method of follow up is video. A video follow-up allows a sales professional to connect with the customer on a more personal level, as the customer can see and hear the salesperson in real time. This can be particularly powerful in helping to establish trust and build a relationship with the customer. Also,

CHAPTER 16

5 Steps to Becoming the Ultimate Closer

DEVELOP A CUSTOMER-FOCUSED AP-PROACH

This can include improving your techniques in the areas of listening to the customer, understanding their needs, and presenting solutions that meet those needs.

OVERCOME OBJECTIONS

Develop your toolbox of strategies for addressing common objections, such as price and availability, and turning them into opportunities to close the deal.

BUILD RAPPORT AND TRUST

Work on your ability to establish a personal connection with the customer and build trust through transparency and honesty.

DEVELOP PERSUASIVE COMMUNICATION

Practice using language and body language effectively to persuade the customer and close the deal.

PRACTICE FOLLOW-UP AND AFTER-SALES SUPPORT

Develop strategies for maintaining contact with the customer after the sale and providing support to ensure their satisfaction and loyalty.

The salespeople with the skills and knowledge to effectively close deals and build lasting relationships with customers become the master closers.

Additional Strategies

OUT-WORK AND OUT-IMPROVE

Continuously improving and learning is essential for success as a master closer in the automotive industry. Here are some steps you can take to ensure success in this area:

SEEK OUT PROFESSIONAL DEVELOPMENT OPPORTUNITIES

Look for training programs or workshops that can help you improve your skills and knowledge in the automotive industry. This could include sales training, product knowledge training, or leadership development programs.

STAY UP TO DATE ON INDUSTRY TRENDS

Keep an eye on industry news and developments to ensure that you have a current and relevant understanding of the automotive market. This could include reading industry publications, attending conferences or events, or following industry leaders on social media.

LEARN FROM OTHERS

Seek out opportunities to learn from more experienced colleagues or mentors by asking for feedback on your sales techniques, shadowing more successful salespeople, or participating in team-building activities.

PRACTICE AND REFINE YOUR SKILLS

To continually improve, it's important to practice and refine your skills through role-playing with colleagues, seeking out sales opportunities outside of work, or setting goals for yourself and tracking your progress.

TAKE TIME TO REFLECT

Make time to reflect on your successes and challenges as a salesperson by keeping a journal or having regular check-ins with a manager or mentor to discuss your progress and areas for improvement.

By taking these steps and being proactive about your professional development, you can ensure that you are continuously improving and learning, which is essential for success as a master closer.

Weekly Strategy to Fast-Track Your Journey to Becoming a Master Closer:

WEEK 1

DEVELOP A CUSTOMER-FOCUSED AP-PROACH IN AUTOMOTIVE SALES

In today's competitive automotive market, it's more important than ever to develop a customer-focused approach. This means understanding the customer's needs and providing solutions that meet those needs. By doing so, you can not only close more deals but also build lasting relationships with customers and retain their loyalty.

Strategies for Developing a Customer-Focused Approach

LISTEN ACTIVELY AND EMPATHIZE WITH THE CUSTOMER

To understand the customer's needs, you need to listen to them carefully and try to see things from their perspective. This means asking open-ended questions, using active listening techniques, and showing empathy for the customer's situation.

PRESENT SOLUTIONS THAT ARE TAILORED TO THE CUSTOMER'S NEEDS

Once you have a clear understanding of the customer's needs, you can present solutions that are tailored to those needs. This could include highlighting the features and benefits of your product or service that are most relevant to the customer and explaining how they can solve the customer's problems or meet their needs.

FOLLOW UP AND PROVIDE AFTER-SALES SUPPORT

It's important to maintain contact with the customer *after* the sale and provide support to ensure their satisfaction and loyalty. This could include following up with the customer to check in on their experience, providing after-sales vehicle service support, and handling any complaints or concerns that arise. This makes sales number 2 and 3 happen.

OVERCOME OBJECTIONS

As an automotive salesperson, you will inevitably encounter objections from customers. These concerns may be related to price, availability, or the suitability of a specific product or service for the customer's needs. It's important to be prepared to address these objections and turn them into opportunities to close the deal.

Key Strategies for Overcoming Objections

ANTICIPATE COMMON OBJECTIONS

Before meeting with the customer, think about the common objections you've encountered or been warned about in the areas of price, availability, or the competition. By anticipating these objections, you can prepare responses that address the customer's concerns and help move the conversation forward.

LISTEN TO THE CUSTOMER AND UNDER-STAND THEIR PERSPECTIVE

When the customer raises an objection, listen carefully and try to understand their perspective. This will help you tailor your response and address their concerns in a way that is meaningful to them.

TURN OBJECTIONS INTO OPPORTUNITIES

Instead of seeing objections as obstacles, try to see them as opportunities to demonstrate the value of your product or service. For example, if the customer raises a concern about price, you could explain the unique features and benefits of your product that make it worth the investment.

MIRROR THE CUSTOMER

Mirroring the customer is an FBI negotiation trick that's the closest thing to a "jedi mind trick," according to Chris Voss, author of Never Split the Difference. Mirroring is the simple repetition of one to three words, typically the last one to three words someone said. When this approach is employed, the other person feels listened to. It tends to connect their thoughts in their head, and it's a way to help flesh out objections. It sends a message to the other person that said, "I heard every word you said, word for word, and I'm proving it by repeating it back to you." When people provide further explanation, they're going to add more words. They're going to change their terms, which helps flesh out the real objection. Try it when the customer says, "I want to think about it." Repeating, "I want to think about it" pushes the customer to rephrase the sentence in terms of what exactly they may need to think about.

BUILD RAPPORT AND TRUST

To close deals and retain customers in this industry, it's important to establish a personal connection and build trust. It's critical to create rapport with customers and be transparent and honest with them.

Key Strategies for Building Rapport and Trust

USE OPEN-ENDED QUESTIONS AND MIRROR THE CUSTOMER'S BODY LANGUAGE

In so doing, you create a comfortable connection with them, which makes the customer feel more comfortable and open to your ideas.

BE TRANSPARENT AND HONEST

It's important to be transparent and honest with your customers in order to establish trust. This means being upfront about the features and benefits of your product or service as well as any of its limitations or potential drawbacks.

DEAL WITH DIFFICULT SITUATIONS

Despite your best efforts, you may encounter difficult situations with customers, such as complaints or concerns. It's important to handle these situations in a way that maintains the customer's trust and confidence in you. Apologize sincerely for any mistakes you might make, offer solutions to address the customer's concerns, and follow up to ensure their satisfaction. Don't be afraid to get a manager or team member involved. The key is to build loyalty with you customer base and get them coming back.

PRACTICE PERSUASIVE COMMUNICATION

To close deals in this space, you obviously need to be able to persuade customers to take action. One way of doing this is through using effective verbal language and body language to convince the customer that your product or service is the right choice for them. By mastering the art of persuasive communication, you can increase your sales and build lasting relationships with customers.

Strategies to Improve Your Persuasive Communication Skills

USE LANGUAGE THAT IS CLEAR AND CONCISE

Avoid jargon or technical terms that the customer may not understand. Use simple, straightforward language.

HIGHLIGHT FEATURES AND BENEFITS

Highlight the features and benefits of your product or service that are most relevant to your customer. Perhaps explain more in depth how a specific product or service can solve the customer's problems or meet their needs and provide specific examples to illustrate the value of your product or service.

USE BODY LANGUAGE

Use body language to reinforce your message. In addition to using verbal language effectively, you can also use body language to reinforce your message and persuade the customer. Make eye contact, use open gestures, and lean in to show interest and engagement.

EXECUTE FOLLOW-UP AND AFTER-SALES SUPPORT

After closing a deal, it's important to maintain contact with the customer and provide support to ensure their satisfaction and loyalty. This means following up with the customer to check in on their experience, providing after-sales support, and handling any complaints or concerns that arise.

Key Strategies for Effective Follow-Up and After-Sales Support

EXECUTE THE FOLLOW-UP

After closing the deal, it's important to follow up with the customer to check in on their experience and ensure their satisfaction. Send a thank-you note or email, call to check in, or ask directly for feedback. By following up, you show the customer that you care about their experience and are willing to address any concerns they may have.

PROVIDE AFTER-SALES SUPPORT

In addition to following up, it's important to provide after-sales support to ensure the customer's satisfaction. Provide instructions for using the product or service, answer any questions the customer may have, and offer support for any problems or issues that arise.

HANDLE COMPLAINTS AND CONCERNS EFFECTIVELY

Despite your best efforts, you may encounter complaints or concerns from customers. It's important to handle these situations in a way that maintains the customer's trust and confidence in you. Apologize for any mistakes, offer solutions to address the customer's concerns, and follow up to ensure their satisfaction.

CHAPTER 17

FINAL WORDS

'm grateful to have been able to share with you the many tactical procedures and techniques that have contributed to my own success over the years, as well as the success of the many closers I've trained and worked with.

We've explored the art and science of closing deals in the automotive sector, and we've examined how great salespeople approach objections, develop rapport with customers, and eventually, close deals. We've confirmed that being successful in the market requires more than just charm or product expertise; it also requires a strategic approach, perseverance, and a readiness to learn from failures.

"The Closer" is, ultimately, a book about the power of human connection, not just the mechanics of the sales process. All long-term, mutually beneficial, profitable customer relation-ships prove how crucial it is to establish trust and rapport early on, as well as the positive effect that sincere care and consideration has on a com-pany's bottom line.

In addition to providing you with useful and actionable advice, I hope this book has motivated you to approach your work with greater honesty and empathy. The core message of "The Closer" is a reminder that success in sales (and in life) is not solely dependent on your actions, but also on who you choose to be in each and every interac-tion.

In the next section, I'll provide you with some of the most common objections you're likely to hear as a closer, as well as the rebuttals that have served me and my employees well over the years. There is also ample space for you to consider and jot down additional ways you may hear the objec-tions framed and alternate responses. Being pre-pared and then practicing your knowledgeable, confident, compassionate response over and over again is what will ultimately land you in the position of being a consistently successful closer.

COMMON SALES & FINANCE WORD TRACKS AND OBJECTION HANDLING TECHNIQUES

FINANCING OBJECTIONS

OBJECTION
"I want to pay cash."

REBUTTAL

Interest rates are still historically very low. My job is to save you time and money and show you why it's better to have more cash on hand for the next 36 months than putting up all the money yourself. This finance option will only cost you 5% to debt service this loan annually, and your vehicle depreciates (on average) 20-30% in the first year and 15-18% in years two through six.

Using our financial terms today gives you more flexibility and available cash on hand to invest in appreciating assists versus this vehicle. I just need your initials here to get started showing you options.

Note: Having more cash on hand is a better option for any individual in both good and bad times, as it gives your customer the option to invest in appreciating assets.

PRACTICE WORKING WITH THIS OBJECTION
Write down additional objections you might receive from the rebuttal.

Write down additional rebuttals you may use in response to those possible objections. (Note: You may have to combine several word tracks to overcome the objection.)

OBJECTION
"The payment is too high."
(when the payment is a small amount higher than where they initially expressed a desire to be)

REBUTTAL
I understand how you feel. However, for less than a daily Starbucks coffee each month, you can drive home in your new vehicle today. I just need your signature and date here.

Note: Reducing the price to the ridiculous is a great way to justify your number and help you move forward.

PRACTICE WORKING WITH THIS OBJECTION
Write down additional objections you might receive from the rebuttal.

Write down additional rebuttals you may use in response to those possible objections.

OBJECTION
"The financing term is too long."

REBUTTAL
Mr./Mrs. [insert last name], the extra time doesn't concern me as much as giving you the option to keep your payment low and in line with your budget. This allows you to keep more cash on hand as well as the flexibility to pay more a month, when you can, or pay just the minimum when unexpected expenses come up. I just need your initials here.

Note: Helping the consumer stay on budget will be key in having happy customers who have the long-term protection they need to secure their investment.

PRACTICE WORKING WITH THIS OBJECTION

Write down additional objections you might receive from the rebuttal.

Write down additional rebuttals you may use in response to those possible objections.

OBJECTION

"The interest rate is too high."

REBUTTAL

If you were paying a mortgage, the rate difference would be substantial over a 30-year term. Since you're only going [insert number of months], the interest you'll be paying is marginal. Plus, if you made one extra payment a year, you could essentially pay down the interest and save yourself the interest you would incur.

I recommend moving forward with this term, and if rates do go down in the short term, you can refinance or pay it off sooner, as it's a simple interest loan. I just need your initials here.

Note: Recognize that rates have gone up and build value in the simple interest. Always make the recommendation and ask for the sale.

PRACTICE WORKING WITH THIS OBJECTION

Write down additional objections you might receive from the rebuttal.

Write down additional rebuttals you may use in response to those possible objections.

OBJECTION
"The interest rate is high."
(Customer states that a specific bank has one listed lower)

REBUTTAL

Have you been through their approval process?

Like most advertised prices, they base their offers on 800+ credit scores and shorter-term loans with a heavy equity loan to value.

Will you be able to contribute 30% down to help get my lending institutions to match their offer?

Allow me to show you a similarly attractive offer that won't impact your cash on hand. I just need your initials here.

Note: Fleshing out what you're really competing with will allow you to better help your customer get into the vehicle they want today.

PRACTICE WORKING WITH THIS OBJECTION
Write down additional objections you might receive from the rebuttal.

Write down additional rebuttals you may use in response to those possible objections.

OBJECTION
"I want to use my bank."

REBUTTAL

I can appreciate your loyalty. However, I would be doing you a disservice if I didn't at least show you how we may be able to save you $1,000's long term with our short-term finance options. Because we have access to 40 different lenders our platform gives our customers the leverage to have the lenders compete for your business, to ensure you get the absolute best finance options.

With credit scoring systems, all hard inquires that occur with 14 days of each other are considered as one inquiry for the scoring model. As a result, it's in your best interest to secure the absolute best terms for you I just need your initials here to proceed.

Note: Most consumers are unaware of this and are concerned if they allow a dealer to run their credit again that multiple inquiries will affect them. To put the consumer at ease, google "hard inquires within 14 days" and you will see the results from Equifax, Experian, and Trans Union that will back up this statement.

PRACTICE WORKING WITH THIS OBJECTION

Write down additional objections you might receive from the rebuttal.

Write down additional rebuttals you may use in response to those possible objections.

PRODUCTS OR ADD-ON OBJECTIONS

OBJECTION
"I never do add-on products."

REBUTTAL
Mr./Mrs. [insert name], I can appreciate that. However, I am still obligated to present what is available to you and ensure it's being recorded, because in the event that something does go wrong, we need to have video showing you were presented the products, but you declined. That way, we won't be held liable. Don't worry, I'll show you why most of my customers buy the protection plan.

Note: Always present every product. I've personally been involved in deals where customers play the "I was never offered that" and expect the dealer to pay for it out of pocket. Presenting the options is important to protect yourself, the customer, and the dealer.

PRACTICE WORKING WITH THIS OBJECTION

Write down additional objections you might receive from the rebuttal.

Write down additional rebuttals you may use in response to those possible objections.

OBJECTION

"I don't need to enroll in the service program. I have my own mechanic."

REBUTTAL

That's great! We don't want to hurt a long-lasting relationship. Mechanics are our best customers, as the electrical and ECU works is brought directly to us. So, when you enroll in the service program whatever your mechanic can't do will be covered as well (as what he *can* do). I just need your signature here.

Note: Mechanics do not make the parts. They also don't like to work for free. Reminding the customer of this reality will help sway them to move forward.

PRACTICE WORKING WITH THIS OBJECTION

Write down additional objections you might receive from the rebuttal.

Write down additional rebuttals you may use in response to those possible objections.

OBJECTION

"I'll take the products if you offer a discount."

REBUTTAL 1

Mr./Mrs. [insert name], I can appreciate that you see the value in our products, and I never like to say no to my customers. However, the prices are set. What I can do, however, is tweak the terms a little and move the miles to help you get these products at a more attractive price. You said previously that you drive your vehicles for [insert number] of years. If I move the term down to [insert number] months, the miles down to [insert number] and raise the deductible to [insert number], I can save you [insert dollar amount] per month. I just need your initials here.

Note: Adjusting the terms will allow you to provide great service to your customer without discounting prices.

PRACTICE WORKING WITH THIS OBJECTION

Write down additional objections you might receive from the rebuttal.

Write down additional rebuttals you may use in response to those possible objections.

OBJECTION

"I'll take the products if you offer a discount."

REBUTTAL 2

My goal is to help you save time and money. There are times when we have some coupons available if you are a member of USAA or Costco. Do you happen to be a member? Let me check with my supervisor to see if we have an option for you.

Note: Discounting with purpose is key to presenting yourself as a professional and not looking like an amateur. This is also a good transition if you're stuck in a deal and can't quite get the customer over the finish line. Your options are interchangeable if your store has incentives for teachers, members of law enforcement, active military personnel, nurses, doctors, or credit union members.

PRACTICE WORKING WITH THIS OBJECTION

Write down additional objections you might receive from the rebuttal.

Write down additional rebuttals you may use in response to those possible objections.

OBJECTION
"I don't need a warranty."

REBUTTAL 1

Based on the basic mechanical functions of the vehicle, I would say that you're going to be in good shape as long as you keep your routine maintenance. However, with technology as advanced as it has become, you need protection on the computer programs your vehicle has. With over a million lines of code throughout the vehicle and the extreme temperatures the computer software in your vehicle is exposed to, this extended service contract will reduce that exposure and protect your investment long term. I just need your initials here.

Note: Whenever you start talking about the technology, grab your iPhone and remind them what happens to their phone when it gets hot. This will help you reinforce the need for your customer to move forward with the warranty.

PRACTICE WORKING WITH THIS OBJECTION

Write down additional objections you might receive from the rebuttal.

Write down additional rebuttals you may use in response to those possible objections.

OBJECTION
"I don't need a warranty."

REBUTTAL 2

If you were going to be in a shorter-term loan and going to trade the vehicle in before the warranty expired, I would agree with you. However, since you opted to go long term, your manufacturer's warranty will expire and leave you exposed for the remainder of your loan. This warranty will reduce your exposure. For less than a daily cup of coffee, you can secure your investment and retain more cash on hand in the long term. I just need your initials here.

Note: Using keywords and financial terms to help elevate the customer's awareness can help you keep the deal moving forward. Always assume the sale immediately.

PRACTICE WORKING WITH THIS OBJECTION

Write down additional objections you might receive from the rebuttal.

Write down additional rebuttals you may use in response to those possible objections.

OBJECTION

"I previously had a bad experience with a warranty."

REBUTTAL

I understand. There are some unscrupulous people in our industry who do good people like yourself wrong. However, I've been with ABC motors for [insert number of years], and I value my customers and want to ensure I help guide them to make the best choice that will reduce their exposure of their investment.

This warranty is an exclusionary warranty and cancellable at any time. It's also fully transferable, so if you sell your vehicle in the future, you can sell it with the value of this warranty. This reduces your exposure long term and is something I recommend you move forward with. I just need your initials here.

Note: Empathizing with the consumer about the unscrupulous individuals who work in this industry and reconfirming your position will help you secure your customer's trust and move forward with the deal.

PRACTICE WORKING WITH THIS OBJECTION

Write down additional objections you might receive from the rebuttal.

Write down additional rebuttals you may use in response to those possible objections.

OBJECTION
"I don't need ceramic coating."

REBUTTAL

I would normally agree with you, but I recently saw exactly how the ceramic coating protects your vehicle. With today's ultraviolet B rays, the sun causes the paint to fade at a faster rate than ever before. The ceramic coating bonds and reinforces the paint while creating a shine that can double the life of your paint. It keeps your vehicle looking like it's been waxed any time you wash it, giving you that new-car look for years.

I recommend you protect your vehicle so that when it comes time to trade it in, your vehicle will have that new-car look. Overall, it helps the vehicle hold its value longer. I just need your initials here.

Note: Rebuild value in the product and highlight key points to help you convert. Always recommit the customer immediately afterward.

PRACTICE WORKING WITH THIS OBJECTION

Write down additional objections you might receive from the rebuttal.

Write down additional rebuttals you may use in response to those possible objections.

OBJECTION

"I don't want windshield protection."

REBUTTAL

I understand. No one wants to pay more than they've already agreed to pay. However, knowing the vehicle you purchased and the condition of the roads, I would be remiss if I didn't offer it.

Fourteen million vehicles have their windshields replaced every year, and more than three times that are damaged by rocks and other flying debris. This product also puts a protective coating on your windshield that helps with visibility during rainstorms. I recommend it not only for appearances but also for the safety of you and your family. I just need your initials here.

Note: This is the "empathize-justify" close in action. Showing empathy and building value will help you close the transaction. Don't leave any statement without reconfirming the sale.

PRACTICE WORKING WITH THIS OBJECTION

Write down additional objections you might receive from the rebuttal.

Write down additional rebuttals you may use in response to those possible objections.

OBJECTION
"I don't want tire and wheel coverage."

REBUTTAL
Mr./Mrs. [insert name], I apologize. I didn't explain it properly. My company spent over $1,000,000 in claims last year, so I see firsthand the value that spending the equivalent of less than two lattes a month will save you down the road. 24/7 roadside assistance and tire and wheel replacement at no cost if damage occurs is why all my clients purchase this package. I just need your initials here.

Note: Building value in how many claims your company pays out is key in building confidence in the product. Always ask for the sale immediately after the rebuttal, as this will help you move forward.

PRACTICE WORKING WITH THIS OBJECTION

Write down additional objections you might receive from the rebuttal.

Write down additional rebuttals you may use in response to those possible objections.

OBJECTION

"I don't want the key replacement insurance."

REBUTTAL

I understand, and normally I'd agree with you. However, I recently spoke with my parts manager, and he said we helped save customers over $50,000 last year in key replacements. I was shocked to hear how many people lose their keys! For less than the cost of two cups of coffee each month, you can reduce your chances of having to incur this expense. I just need your initials here.

Note: Check with your parts department on the exact dollar amount, and if you want to take it one step further, print it out to show the customer.

PRACTICE WORKING WITH THIS OBJECTION
Write down additional objections you might receive from the rebuttal.

Write down additional rebuttals you may use in
response to those possible objections.

TRADE-IN OBJECTIONS

OBJECTION
"I received a better trade-in offer for my vehicle at CarMax."

REBUTTAL 1
I understand. If I could get you that offer, I would. However, you are here because my vehicle is $1500 less than theirs. Since I'm saving you money on the total deal, let's move forward. I need your signature and date.

Note: Some clients see the value of their time and will move forward if you ask the right way.

PRACTICE WORKING WITH THIS OBJECTION
Write down additional objections you might receive from the rebuttal.

Write down additional rebuttals you may use in response to those possible objections.

OBJECTION
"I received a better trade-in offer for my vehicle at CarMax."

REBUTTAL 2

Have you been there in person? What we have found is, clients who went online to get their quote and haven't gone in person, the price will change. Did you, by chance, tell them about the damage on the vehicle or the worn tires? I can assure you, if it was a matter of just matching their price, we would. (Or, if these things were taken care of, we would.) I just need your signature and date here and we can move forward.

Note: this does happen and if the Carfax is bad on the vehicle, they can expect the price to drop even further when they arrive at the big box retailer.

PRACTICE WORKING WITH THIS OBJECTION

Write down additional objections you might receive from the rebuttal.

Write down additional rebuttals you may use in response to those possible objections.

OBJECTION

"I want more for my trade."

REBUTTAL

I understand, and we would love to give you more for it were there not $1,000 in damage. Plus, it needs $800 in new tires. Let us do this: since you are financing, let us see if we can save you money on your interest. If we can save you half or one percent on your loan, it would make up the difference. I need your signature and date here.

Note: This is where the silent walkaround is important to identify areas of the vehicle that the dealership will need to pay to recondition. This also allows you to hold on to their trade.

PRACTICE WORKING WITH THIS OBJECTION
Write down additional objections you might receive from the rebuttal.

Write down additional rebuttals you may use in response to those possible objections.

OBJECTION
"I need to sell my car on my own."

REBUTTAL

I understand. I can assure you that is not the best option. Keep in mind, you will have to spend money to list the vehicle on your own. You will have to take strangers on test drives. The average private party sale takes two to three months, and with current market volatility, the consumer makes an average of just $500 more than they were offered from a dealership (after expenses). Your time is worth more than $5 a day, isn't it? I need your signature and date here.

Note: The consumer will be making monthly car payments and insurance payments in addition to advertising expenses and taking time away from their daily life to show the vehicle and get the paperwork done on the sale of the vehicle.

PRACTICE WORKING WITH THIS OBJECTION
Write down additional objections you might receive from the rebuttal.

Write down additional rebuttals you may use in response to those possible objections.

RATE OBJECTIONS

OBJECTION
"I want to use my bank."

REBUTTAL 1

I understand. However, did you know that the payment you will be making could be the same with the banks we use—with one exception: I may be able to get you a warranty included in that payment. This is great news, because you've already pulled your credit with your bank, so your credit won't be further affected. Give me five minutes to prove it to you. Worst case, we can always use your bank.

Note: This approach may take a little more work, as you must show the value of using your bank as opposed to the customer's bank. This approach is perfect to use when people have built a relationship with their bank and are resistant to switching. The idea is to save them one or two points and show them how much they would pay in finance charges over the course of the loan. Have your finance manager provide the option of keeping their payment the same by using their bank (and their bank's higher interest rate). Since their credit has already been pulled, running two different options won't affect their credit further, given that credit companies allow for a 14-day window in which to run a customer's credit for the same type of service to allow them to comparison shop.

Most consumers are unaware of this and are concerned if they allow a dealer to run their credit again that multiple inquiries will affect them. To put the consumer at ease, google "hard inquiries within 14 days" and you will see the results from Equifax, Experian, and Trans Union to back up this statement.

PRACTICE WORKING WITH THIS OBJECTION

Write down additional objections you might receive from the rebuttal.

Write down additional rebuttals you may use in response to those possible objections.

OBJECTION
"I want to use my bank."

REBUTTAL 2
No problem, we have over forty lenders on our lending platform, and chances are, your bank is one of them. The beauty of our platform is that our banks compete for your business, and we've been able to get our customers better rates as a result. Let's begin the application process.

Note: Always assume the next step. Don't get hung up on this "winning" this rebuttal. Chances are, the bigger deal you make it, the longer it will keep you stuck.

PRACTICE WORKING WITH THIS OBJECTION

Write down additional objections you might receive from the rebuttal.

Write down additional rebuttals you may use in response to those possible objections.

OBJECTION
"I don't want you to pull my credit."

REBUTTAL

No problem. Since you're going to be buying soon anyway, the good thing is that the credit bureaus understand that people do shop around, and they allow you to run your credit multiple times within fourteen days with it only counting as one pull. Let's get your application started so we can find out exactly what your payment will be so you can make an educated decision. What's your social security number?

Note: Once you've made this statement, roll right into the credit application. This statement is true. You can confirm it on Equifax or any credit bureau's website.

PRACTICE WORKING WITH THIS OBJECTION
Write down additional objections you might receive from the rebuttal.

Write down additional rebuttals you may use in response to those possible objections.

OBJECTION
"What's your best rate?"

REBUTTAL

I unfortunately cannot tell you what the bank will determine your best rate is until we get you to the next step. I, for one, have seen some people get as low as 0% on some cars, but that's not on every car. I could tell you other rates I've seen some customers get because after putting 50% down. Your rate will be based on a few different factors, and it only takes a couple of minutes to find out what the result is. Let's go ahead and get your application started. What's your social security number?

Note: As you're saying this, you can immediately reach for an application or start the process of filling out the application online. Assume that the next step will proceed as you'd like it to.

PRACTICE WORKING WITH THIS OBJECTION

Write down additional objections you might receive from the rebuttal.

Write down additional rebuttals you may use in response to those possible objections.

OBJECTION
"I have bad credit."

REBUTTAL

No Problem! We have a New Beginnings program that allows customers in similar situations to get re-established. We know that bad things happen to good people, and we have some finance options for people in your situation. Let's get a credit application started.

Note: Although finance options are solely at the lender's discretion, this approach will help you get the customer to the next step to determine how you can best help them.

PRACTICE WORKING WITH THIS OBJECTION

Write down additional objections you might receive from the rebuttal.

Write down additional rebuttals you may use in response to those possible objections.

OBJECTION
"The rate is too high."

REBUTTAL

I understand. Compared to what you would have paid had the Federal Reserve not raised interest rates, I agree. However, this is a simple interest loan, so you can pay it off earlier and save yourself the $0.50 a day increase it will cost you in interest to take this vehicle home today. I just need your signature and date here. By the way, when did you want your payments to start? The middle or the end of the month?

Note: Reduce the objection to the ridiculous. This works, as most consumers know that the Fed has raised interest rates. Keep moving the deal forward and ask for the sale.

PRACTICE WORKING WITH THIS OBJECTION

Write down additional objections you might receive from the rebuttal.

Write down additional rebuttals you may use in response to those possible objections.

OBJECTION

"That rate is too high."
(assuming the customer has good credit)

REBUTTAL

I understand. The difference between an auto loan and a home loan is, the auto loan is short term, and a half percent difference will only cost about $300 in interest, whereas with a home loan, that difference might cost you several thousand dollars. I need your signature and date here.

Note: You may have to break the numbers down further. The point is to acknowledge it and move on. A typical pitfall is sticking with this complaint and thinking it's an objection instead of a simple complaint. Doing this often ends up costing the salesperson money.

PRACTICE WORKING WITH THIS OBJECTION

Write down additional objections you might receive from the rebuttal.

Write down additional rebuttals you may use in response to those possible objections.

OBJECTION

"That rate is too high."
(assuming the customer has bad credit)

REBUTTAL

I understand. What I recommend my clients do in your position is, take this loan on for consecutive months. This allows you to re-establish your credit by using a retail installment loan for at least twelve months. This will help increase your credit score (as long as you make your payments on time) and give you an opportunity to refinance in thirteen months at your bank or credit union. We can also trade you out of this vehicle and get you into a newer one at that time. I need your signature and date here.

Note: This approach is highly effective and short-ens the timeframe for the consumer to come back to see you to help them get another deal.

PRACTICE WORKING WITH THIS OBJECTION

Write down additional objections you might receive from the rebuttal.

Write down additional rebuttals you may use in response to those possible objections.

PRICE OBJECTIONS

OBJECTION
"Carmax has one cheaper."

REBUTTAL

Mr./Mrs. Customer, the difference between our vehicle and theirs is that when we certified ours, we took it through the manufacturer's standards. For example, when we look at tires, we have to ensure that all four tires match. They don't. That's why the warranty that comes with our CPO lasts longer.

Details like this will allow your vehicle to last longer. So, while on the surface you might feel like you're paying more, long term this vehicle will last longer. I just need your signature and date here.

Note: Building value in our OEM Certification is key. Keep in mind that most OEM Certifications also come with a longer basic warranty than Car-Max's 90-day, 4,000-mile warranty.

PRACTICE WORKING WITH THIS OBJECTION

Write down additional objections you might receive from the rebuttal.

Write down additional rebuttals you may use in
response to those possible objections.

OBJECTION

"I don't want to pay the doc fee."

REBUTTAL

I know how you feel. Just like taxes, no one wants to pay it. This fee goes into ensuring your information is safe long term. I need your signature and date here.

Note: We've all heard of the cyber-attacks that have cost companies hundreds of millions of dollars. Acknowledging this common customer concern will help you keep moving forward!

PRACTICE WORKING WITH THIS OBJECTION

Write down additional objections you might receive from the rebuttal.

Write down additional rebuttals you may use in response to those possible objections.

OBJECTION
"I need $500 off the price."

REBUTTAL
I understand. If I had the money to take it off, I would. I just need your signature and date here to move forward.

Note: Most of the time, if you acknowledge, ignore, and move on, you can close the deal without turning it into more than just a complaint.

PRACTICE WORKING WITH THIS OBJECTION
Write down additional objections you might receive from the rebuttal.

Write down additional rebuttals you may use in response to those possible objections.

OBJECTION
"I don't have a downpayment."

REBUTTAL
No problem. We have an option where we will hold a check for up to ten days to allow you to get the money together. I need your signature and date here.

Note: This can be effective. However, if they truly don't have any money to put down, this is a good time to ask for a co-app or a junk trade. Lots of times, customers have an old car in their driveway that can help them and you close the deal.

PRACTICE WORKING WITH THIS OBJECTION

Write down additional objections you might receive from the rebuttal.

Write down additional rebuttals you may use in response to those possible objections.

OBJECTION

"ABC Motors isn't charging over sticker."

REBUTTAL

I understand. I don't like to feel like I'm paying more than I have to, either. However, we don't charge over MSRP on everything. Some vehicles are getting those markups due to supply and demand, while others are being discounted. That dealer doesn't have any in stock and you'll likely be waiting six months to get it exactly how you want it. I can assure you we would advertise no markups as well if we didn't have a handful in stock.

The good thing is, today your vehicle is worth at least $5,000 more than it was a year ago, so it's all relative. I just need your initials here, and we can get this vehicle ready for delivery.

Note: Empathize with the consumer, justify your price, and move on. Practice this until it becomes fluid so that each and every time it comes up, you're ready.

PRACTICE WORKING WITH THIS OBJECTION

Write down additional objections you might receive from the rebuttal.

Write down additional rebuttals you may use in response to those possible objections.

OBJECTION
"The payment is out of my budget."

REBUTTAL
I understand. What if I could help you find a less expensive car insurance payment to help you stay on budget? Who is your insurance through?

Note: This approach can be highly effective. Most people stay with their insurance for way too long, and oftentimes you can help them lower their monthly payment by $30-$50 a month to help them stay in their budget instead of lowering your margin.

PRACTICE WORKING WITH THIS OBJECTION

Write down additional objections you might receive from the rebuttal.

Write down additional rebuttals you may use in response to those possible objections.

OBJECTION
"Is that your best price?"

REBUTTAL 1
The short answer is yes. As you know, the internet has made everything transparent. With companies like CarMax and Carvana and their "no haggle" pricing, we can no longer charge more for our vehicles. In fact, we are, on average, $1500 *below* their price. I need your signature and date here to move forward.

PRACTICE WORKING WITH THIS OBJECTION
Write down additional objections you might receive from the rebuttal.

Write down additional rebuttals you may use in response to those possible objections.

OBJECTION
"Is that your best price?"

REBUTTAL 2

We spend over $20,000 a year in software to ensure we have our best prices listed. There's a reason you picked our vehicle online. It's not because we're the most expensive; it's because it was the best price with the best value. I just need your signature and date here.

Note: People have been trained to ask for the best price. They ask almost to test you to see if there is room to budge. The idea with this rebuttal is to acknowledge, ignore, and move on to close the deal. Telling customers what they already think and then taking it a step further and printing out the same vehicle at another location is a great way to use third-party information to hold your price and assume the sale.

PRACTICE WORKING WITH THIS OBJECTION

Write down additional objections you might receive from the rebuttal.

Write down additional rebuttals you may use in response to those possible objections.

OBJECTION
"The price is too high."

REBUTTAL
I'm sorry to hear that you feel that way. I felt the same way when I bought my car. I've found that our team spends hours each day ensuring that our prices are competitive in the marketplace, so you can take comfort knowing that you are not overpaying. I need your signature and date here.

Note: The "feel, felt, found" method works well in acknowledging and showing empathy of a customer's complaint, moving past it, and assuming the sale.

PRACTICE WORKING WITH THIS OBJECTION
Write down additional objections you might receive from the rebuttal.

Write down additional rebuttals you may use in response to those possible objections.

OBJECTION
"The price is too high."

REBUTTAL 2

I understand. Statistics tell me there is a 90% chance you went online before you came in, so you knew what the price was before you arrived. I need your signature and date here.

Note: This approach is only for sales professionals who have built enough rapport with a customer, and it is to be said while smiling. Understand that—most of the time—this statement by a customer is not an objection but rather a complaint. The goal is to acknowledge, ignore, and move on. Assume the sale.

PRACTICE WORKING WITH THIS OBJECTION

Write down additional objections you might receive from the rebuttal.

Write down additional rebuttals you may use in response to those possible objections.

OBJECTION
"The payment is too high."

REBUTTAL 1

I understand how you feel, and you know what? You are no different than everyone else who comes in. In fact, there was a study done on this a few years ago that found that the average consumer ends up paying $60 more a month than they anticipated. I need your signature and date here.

Note: By using "keeping up with the Joneses" discussions or other forms of social proof makes it easier for you to help the customer justify the purchase and helps you make the sale.

PRACTICE WORKING WITH THIS OBJECTION

Write down additional objections you might receive from the rebuttal.

Write down additional rebuttals you may use in response to those possible objections.

OBJECTION
"The payment is too high."

REBUTTAL 2

I understand. Let's do this: since the banks only lend consumers what they can afford based on their income, let's see what approval the bank gives you. If they approve you, it means they are confident allowing you to purchase this vehicle based on your income and we can move forward. I just need your signature and date here.

Note: Using the bank as third-party confirmation is ideal in situations where clients may have more challenging credit.

PRACTICE WORKING WITH THIS OBJECTION

Write down additional objections you might receive from the rebuttal.

Write down additional rebuttals you may use in response to those possible objections.

STALL OBJECTIONS

OBJECTION
"I have a party to go to. I'm already running late."

REBUTTAL
Awesome! Do me a favor: let's get the car ready for you to take with you. When everyone sees you in your new car, give them my card and tell them who's helping you. I'll have the paperwork ready for you when you get back. I just need a copy of your driver's license and insurance card.

Note: Pending your dealership's borrowed car policy, this is a form of the "puppy dog" close. The goal is for your customer to fall in love with the vehicle and show all their friends and relatives, after which point they won't want to return it. Offer to take the paperwork to them if your dealership allows it.

PRACTICE WORKING WITH THIS OBJECTION

Write down additional objections you might receive from the rebuttal.

Write down additional rebuttals you may use in response to those possible objections.

OBJECTION
"I need to go grab lunch."

REBUTTAL
"Great! Where are you going?" (Allow them to reply). Follow with, "That sounds good! I'll tell you what, I haven't had lunch yet. Why don't I take you and it will be my treat? That way I can go over more details on your new vehicle."

Note: This only works if you've done your job in building rapport with the customer. Sometimes, you'll have to stay in the game with them longer to ensure you close the deal. Going with the customer works well even when the customer doesn't have their title, stipulations, trade, etc.

PRACTICE WORKING WITH THIS OBJECTION

Write down additional objections you might receive from the rebuttal.

Write down additional rebuttals you may use in response to those possible objections.

OBJECTION

"I need to speak to my spouse."

REBUTTAL

I understand. If your spouse is like mine, they know you're here and why. Would they say no to the product or the financial commitment? (If they say that their spouse would have a possible objection to the product, ask what they would suggest as an alternative.

If they say that they anticipate the money being an issue, ask whether the problem will be the trade payment/downpayment or the price.) Then, follow up with "So, what you're saying is, if I could get to where you want to be, we can move forward? I need your signature and date here."

Note: You need to flesh out the real objection. Oftentimes, simply allowing the spouse to drive/see the vehicle will help you keep moving forward in the process. Always recommit the consumer and ask for the sale.

PRACTICE WORKING WITH THIS OBJECTION
Write down additional objections you might receive from the rebuttal.

Write down additional rebuttals you may use in response to those possible objections.

OBJECTION

"I want to wait for my insurance check."

REBUTTAL

Do you know if the vehicle has been deemed a total loss? If it has, then chances are you don't have to wait. All we need is the total loss letter. If you have GAP insurance, we can move forward with the deal.

Note: Check with your lender, as what they are looking for is whether the customer has a deficiency balance and is going to have trouble making the payments. Many times, all you need is the total loss letter and original gap contract, and you can make the deal.

PRACTICE WORKING WITH THIS OBJECTION
Write down additional objections you might receive from the rebuttal.

Write down additional rebuttals you may use in response to those possible objections.

OBJECTION

"I'm going to wait."

REBUTTAL

I understand. However, taking more time to make a decision will not make your decision any easier. There are three things you will have to decide: Do you like the people you are buying from? Do you like the vehicle? Is the money right? What I mean is, what part of the money doesn't make sense. Is it the down payment, the trade, or the price? After that, it sounds like you have everything you need to make a decision. I need your signature and date here.

Note: What you're doing here is trying to flesh out the real objection. Always assume the sale if they've answered yes to all questions. A typical pitfall is spending too much time addressing one specific complaint.

PRACTICE WORKING WITH THIS OBJECTION
Write down additional objections you might receive from the rebuttal.

Write down additional rebuttals you may use in
response to those possible objections.

OBJECTION
"I want to think about it."

REBUTTAL 1
You need to think about it?

Note: Mirroring your customer by repeating the exact same thing they said to you in an inquisitive way (and immediately pausing for them to re-spond) can help you flesh out the real objection. Doing this with any objection is a great way to help you get to the root of the objection.

PRACTICE WORKING WITH THIS OBJECTION

Write down additional objections you might receive from the rebuttal.

Write down additional rebuttals you may use in
response to those possible objections.

OBJECTION
"I want to think about it."

REBUTTAL 2

Mr./Mrs. Customer, the vehicle you're looking at has the exact options and features you indicated you wanted. The payment falls inline and within your budget. Doesn't it make sense to move forward? All we need is your signature and date, and we'll get your vehicle cleaned and ready for delivery (at this point, hand them the pen to sign the write up).

Note: All too often, we hear this objection and stop. Simply reconfirming what the customer already knows while assuming the sale often gets them over the finish line.

PRACTICE WORKING WITH THIS OBJECTION
Write down additional objections you might receive from the rebuttal.

Write down additional rebuttals you may use in
response to those possible objections.

OBJECTION
"I want to think about it."

REBUTTAL 3

I understand. Let's go ahead and get you signed up today. We will allow you to take the vehicle home with you, and if you wake up tomorrow feeling like you made a mistake, just bring the car back and we will unwind the deal. I need your signature and date here.

Note: Pending your dealership's return policy, this is a form of the "puppy dog" Close." The goal is for them to fall in love with the vehicle and show all their friends and relatives, so they don't want to return it.

PRACTICE WORKING WITH THIS OBJECTION
Write down additional objections you might receive from the rebuttal.

Write down additional rebuttals you may use in response to those possible objections.

OBJECTION
"I want to think about it."

REBUTTAL 4

Absolutely. Better yet, let's move forward so you can see all the paperwork you will receive from our finance department as well. This will allow you to drive the vehicle home and if, for whatever reason, you decide this vehicle doesn't fit your needs, we can take the car back and tear up the agreement. I just need your signature and date here.

Note: This approach is only used if your store has a return policy. The idea is to get the customer to fall in love with the vehicle and show it to friends and family so they won't want to return it.

PRACTICE WORKING WITH THIS OBJECTION
Write down additional objections you might receive from the rebuttal.

Write down additional rebuttals you may use in response to those possible objections.

OBJECTION
"I want to think about it."

REBUTTAL 5

I understand that this is a big decision, and I haven't given you enough information. Why don't we get you the necessary information to take home with you so you can make an educated decision. Follow me.

Note: This is a way to help you move forward in the process in order to get to the write up.

PRACTICE WORKING WITH THIS OBJECTION

Write down additional objections you might receive from the rebuttal.

Write down additional rebuttals you may use in response to those possible objections.

OBJECTION
"I'm just looking."

REBUTTAL
Great! Most people love to do that! In fact, we know that, statistically, most people don't buy the first day. This is why we have an information day. This way, we can appraise your vehicle and give you all the information you need to take home and make an educated decision. How does that sound? Follow me!

Note: This approach allows you to keep moving forward and helps you get further along in the process.

PRACTICE WORKING WITH THIS OBJECTION

Write down additional objections you might receive from the rebuttal.

Write down additional rebuttals you may use in response to those possible objections.

OBJECTION
"I still have more shopping to do."

REBUTTAL

I understand, however I don't get paid if you leave. What will it take to earn your business today?

Note: Whatever they offer get it in writing and have them sign. This is the last-ditch effort and should only be used at the last resort. This is usually overused by green and undertrained salespeople.

PRACTICE WORKING WITH THIS OBJECTION
Write down additional objections you might receive from the rebuttal.

Write down additional rebuttals you may use in response to those possible objections.

OBJECTION
"I still need to shop around a bit more."

REBUTTAL
I understand. What we can do for you is agree to terms and get you on your way. If you find a price less than ours, we will cut you a check back for the difference. I need your signature and date here.

Note: Price guarantees are ideal in a situation where the customer is comparing the same vehicle at different locations.

PRACTICE WORKING WITH THIS OBJECTION

Write down additional objections you might receive from the rebuttal.

Write down additional rebuttals you may use in response to those possible objections.

OBJECTION
"It's a big decision."

REBUTTAL

I agree. When making tough decisions, one of our founding fathers, Ben Franklin, used to make a chart to help him decide. On one side, he would write the pros and the other side he would write cons. He made his decision based on whichever list was longer. Let's try and see what we can produce.

Note: This approach works especially well if you've taken great notes during the needs assessment. It gives you an opportunity to highlight all the reasons they stated they should be buying this vehicle.

PRACTICE WORKING WITH THIS OBJECTION
Write down additional objections you might receive from the rebuttal.

Write down additional rebuttals you may use in response to those possible objections.

OBJECTION
"I don't want to make a rash decision."

REBUTTAL

I understand. A rash decision is one made quickly without and thought. Do you think we've found the features that you've wanted on your new vehicle? Are you happy with your experience so far? Does this payment fit within your budget? Sounds like you've made a rational decision! I just need your signature and date here.

Note: Reclarifying the deal gives the consumer reassurance that they are making a good decision. Assuming the sale in this instance usually gives them the nudge they need to close the deal.

PRACTICE WORKING WITH THIS OBJECTION

Write down additional objections you might receive from the rebuttal.

Write down additional rebuttals you may use in response to those possible objections.

OBJECTION

"If the car is still here tomorrow, then it was meant to be."

REBUTTAL

I understand. Most people who say that go home to decide whether they want to move forward based on three things. One, do I like the sales professional or dealership? Two, is the vehicle I drove the one I want? Three, is this the price I am willing to pay, or is the payment in line with what I want to pay? (Wait for them to answer each question). I just need your signature and date here.

Note: What you're really asking is, "If I can get [insert dollar amount] for your trade or [insert dollar amount] off the car we can earn your business today?" You're trying to flesh out the real objection. Once you've fleshed out the objection, always recommit the consumer and ask for the sale.

PRACTICE WORKING WITH THIS OBJECTION

Write down additional objections you might receive from the rebuttal.

Write down additional rebuttals you may use in response to those possible objections.

OBJECTION
"I want to pray on it."

REBUTTAL

I understand, and I think you should. This reminds me of a story a pastor once told about a man who was lost at sea. A small tugboat passed by and offered to save him. He replied, "No, God will save me." A second, much bigger boat passed and again offered to help, and the man replied, "No God will save me." A third boat passed, this time a cruise ship, and offered to save him. He replied, "No God will save me." The man ended up dying and upon reaching heaven, asked God, "Why didn't you save me?" God replied, "I sent you three boats.'"

Mr./Mrs. [insert customer's last name], you are not here by chance, and I believe God brought you here to meet me. Let 's sign you up today and get you going. If, for whatever reason, you wake up tomorrow and don't like the car, you can return the vehicle and we will tear up the contract. I need your signature here and date here.

Note: This is a more advanced close. If you have not built enough rapport with the customer, it will likely be hard to deliver this close without offending the customer.

PRACTICE WORKING WITH THIS OBJECTION

Write down additional objections you might receive from the rebuttal.

Write down additional rebuttals you may use in response to those possible objections.

GENERAL OBJECTIONS

OBJECTION

"Is the vehicle available?"
(asked when it's not)

REBUTTAL

I'm glad you asked. The [insert vehicle model] is one of our best-selling models. Who's the lucky one that will be getting this vehicle? Do you need this right away, or do we have some time? What drew you to that vehicle? What features are important to you? If I found a pre-owned vehicle with similar options and a comparable price and mileage, would you be open to that option?

Note: The key is to switch them to another vehicle you have in stock. Remember, 85% of all customers who buy end up buying something other than the vehicle they initially came in for.

PRACTICE WORKING WITH THIS OBJECTION
Write down additional objections you might receive from the rebuttal.

Write down additional rebuttals you may use in response to those possible objections.

OBJECTION
"The vehicle has high miles."

REBUTTAL
(Depending on the vehicle) These vehicles are rated to go over 150,000 (domestic)/250,000 (import) miles. Even better news: we have warranties that will reduce your exposure for the life of the loan. Let's take this vehicle for a test drive, and I'll show you how this vehicle will end up being well below your budget.

Note: With vehicles lasting longer and longer, most clients don't realize how long vehicles are rated to last.

PRACTICE WORKING WITH THIS OBJECTION

Write down additional objections you might receive from the rebuttal.

Write down additional rebuttals you may use in response to those possible objections.

OBJECTION
"I just don't like the color."

REBUTTAL

Would you be willing to go color blind for a heck of a deal? We are in the business of making deals today. Let's get you to the next step so you can see what kind of deal we can make you on this vehicle. Follow me.

Note: Customers will sometimes buy the deal instead of the color. This approach is helped me sell numerous cars over the years.

PRACTICE WORKING WITH THIS OBJECTION

Write down additional objections you might receive from the rebuttal.

Write down additional rebuttals you may use in response to those possible objections.

OBJECTION

Any general objection (when you need a Hail Mary)

REBUTTAL

I want to apologize. I wasn't able to help you move forward today. But I have to ask you, what will it take to earn your business today? (Write down whatever they say.) So, what you're saying is, if I can do _____, I can earn your business today? Perfect, I just need your signature and date here.

Note: This rebuttal is used as a last resort. Be careful because this close can cost you gross. Don't use this unless it's absolutely necessary.

PRACTICE WORKING WITH THIS OBJECTION

Write down additional objections you might receive from the rebuttal.

Write down additional rebuttals you may use in response to those possible objections.

OBJECTION

Any objection having to do with another party,
when the party who will be assisting the
customer is unavailable

REBUTTAL

No problem. Let's move forward, pending
their approval, and let you take the vehicle home
with you. I just need your signature and date
here.

Note: This approach works as long as your dealership has a return policy.

PRACTICE WORKING WITH THIS OBJECTION

Write down additional objections you might receive from the rebuttal.

Write down additional rebuttals you may use in response to those possible objections.

OBJECTION

Any objection when it seems that a third party is involved (who is physically present)

REBUTTAL

Will you be able to help with the down payment, expenses, or financing?

Note: This approach is used either to confirm assistance for the customer or encourage the second baseman to stop interfering.

PRACTICE WORKING WITH THIS OBJECTION

Write down additional objections you might receive from the rebuttal.

Write down additional rebuttals you may use in response to those possible objections.

GREAT T-O OPPORTUNITIES

OBJECTION
"I need to go to a meeting."

REBUTTAL
Before you go, give me five minutes to give you more information to take home with you. That way you can review all the information at home to make a good sound decision. Follow me.

Note: Take the customer to the office and reclarify the deal. If you haven't given them numbers on the trade and/or the vehicle they are buying, get the information to them and assume the sale. Worst case, ensure you give them numbers that will ensure they come back.

PRACTICE WORKING WITH THIS OBJECTION

Write down additional objections you might receive from the rebuttal.

Write down additional rebuttals you may use in response to those possible objections.

OBJECTION

Use when the customer is leaving or already out the door, but the salesperson didn't give you the heads up ("Flying TO")

REBUTTAL

What happened? I apologize, we made a mistake... (Allow the customer to answer.) I understand. What if I can save you $500? Would you stay and do business with us? Follow me.

Note: This is how you get a customer who's left the dealership back inside. This must be said with a smile and enthusiasm. Use the "flying to" when the customer is either at their car or walking to the door and the manager has to "fly to" them to get them back into the office to close the deal.

PRACTICE WORKING WITH THIS OBJECTION
Write down additional objections you might receive from the rebuttal.

Write down additional rebuttals you may use in response to those possible objections.

ABOUT THE AUTHOR

Chris Martinez first entered into the auto sales sector in 2003. Despite having great mentors, he had to forge his own route. He focused on becoming the top seller at his dealership because of his strong sense of faith and family. By working hard and remaining persistent, he not only succeeded in achieving that objective but also went on to publish six bestselling books that have aided salespeople nationwide in enhancing their abilities and advancing their careers.

- *The Unfair Advantage: Digital Marketing Principles That Will Explode the Growth of an Auto Dealership*
- *Driving Sales: What It Takes to Sell 1,000 Cars A Month*
- *The Drive to 30: Your Ultimate Guide to Selling More Cars Than Ever*
- *The Rainmaker: Fundamentals of the Car Dealer's Desk Manager*
- *Digital Marketing Blueprint: A Car Dealer's Guide to Selling More Cars*
- *When I Grow Up, I Want To Be a Car Salesperson!*

Having also founded TheAutoMiner.com, Chris is

currently the Executive Director of sales and marketing at Jackie Cooper Imports of Tulsa. He's spent the last 20 years perfecting his abilities and building successful teams. He's played a crucial part in the opening of five dealerships across the United States, provided important direction for dealership implementation, and turned a troubled single-point store into one of the top ten dealerships in the country.

Chris has established himself as an industry leader with his demonstrated ability to increase sales and profitability, turn around underperforming operations, and implement innovative processes. He believes that striving for perfection, treating others with respect, and working hard leads to success in sales.

Chris is dedicated to educating owners, general managers, dealership managers, and salespeople on how to consistently approach customers in a way that enables them to achieve beyond their marketing and sales goals as he assists the upcoming generation of sales professionals in succeeding and realizing their full potential through his writing and trainings.

Visit CarSalesSuccess.com for more information.

Driving Sales: What It Takes to Sell 1,000+ Cars Per Month is a thorough manual for advancing your auto sales career. With more than 20 years in the business, Chris offers his tips for selling 1000+ cars every month. His career has seen him successfully open five dealerships and turn a failing store into a Top 10 dealership in the US. Anyone working in the automobile industry should read this insider's handbook since it covers subjects including creating a successful sales team, developing the art of closing transactions, and increasing dealership traffic. The methodologies in

Driving Sales helped contribute to a 700% rise in sales at a single point store.

Available online at Amazon.com

The Drive to 30: Your Ultimate Guide to Selling More Cars Than Ever offers a thorough strategy for securing market dominance in the auto industry. Martinez outlines the techniques and strategies to meet sales goals and prevent common pitfalls based on his experience as a former 30-car-per-month salesperson and successful dealership manager. This manual provides you with the information and abilities you need to stand out in the cut-throat auto sales market, including the 4 keys to successful sales, the 10 steps of a winning sales process, recommendations on raising visibility, and how to master sales follow-ups. Don't pass up the potential to sell more automobiles than ever.

Available online at Amazon.com

The Unfair Advantage: Digital Marketing Principles that Will Explode the Growth of an Auto Dealership details the tried-and-true strategy Charles Maund Toyota Dealership used to grow by 700% in just 7 years. This book will teach you how important branding and humanizing your dealership is, the crucial area most dealerships miss, how to create a strong and scalable marketing strategy, and typical traps to watch out for. This repeatable and scalable strategy will put you in a position for long-term growth whether you're an owner, general manager, member of the marketing team, or salesperson. Get *The Unfair Advantage* to avoid having your dealership fall behind.

Available online at Amazon.com

The Rainmaker: Fundamentals of the Car Dealer's
Desk Manager is for desk managers who are prepared to advance their dealership. This pocket
handbook is a potent tool. Find out what it takes
to be the best at strategy, how to get your sales
staff to think alike, how to perform a perfect turn,
and how to get the most of your service bay. Dis-
cover 6 useful strategies for finding excellent offers, avoid common traps, and learn persuasive
ways to sell a deal to lenders. It's time to get this
thorough manual in your hands if you're ready to
start making it rain.

Available online at Amazon.com

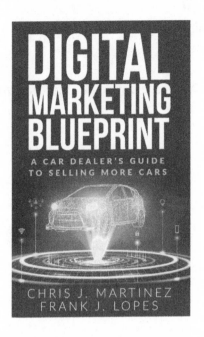

Digital Marketing Blueprint: A Car Dealer's Guide to Selling More Cars is a tried-and-true manual for digital marketing in the automotive space. Due to the rising expense and effectiveness of traditional marketing strategies, many dealers feel helpless, separated from the digital world. With experience of more than 20 years (Chris) and 42 years (Frank) in the automotive industry and a proven track record of success in generating revenue for numerous dealerships, the authors are well-qualified to do so. By embracing the power of digital marketing with the help of this thorough guide, dealerships may succeed in the digital era and join them.

Available online at Amazon.com

When I Grow Up, I Want to Be a Car Salesperson takes you on an amazing trip with Chris and his kids, Jazmin, Janelle, Julianna, and Christian, where bedtime tales transform into a meaningful lesson on discovering one's passion and purpose. This endearing story begins when Chris decides to read a book about a little boy who aspires to be a firefighter, only to encourage his kids to consider their own future goals. The youngsters can't wait to tell their dad what they want to be the next day, and the story finishes with a touching twist that will inspire your kids to pursue their own aspirations. With its cheerful pictures, uplifting sentiments, and endearing characters, this book is an excellent choice for young children who enjoy bedtime stories.

Available online at Amazon.com

The Car Sales Success Closing Drills were created exclusively for Finance Managers and Automotive Sales Professionals to improve their performance and rise to the top. These flashcards offer tested word lists that have previously benefited countless salespeople around the country. Car Sales Success Closing Drills will assist you if you are having trouble closing sales or having trouble as a finance manager. The 108 objections and closing procedures covered by the flashcards are cutting-edge methods from professionals like Chris J. Martinez, Frank J. Lopes, and Adam Marburger. The Car Sales Success Closing Drills flashcards offer the training and mastery required to assist you in closing more deals.

Available at CarSalesSuccess.com

The Car Sales Success app, which is accessible on the App Store, offers a complete solution for people who want to excel in the auto sales sector. The app provides a variety of materials and tools, such as flashcards, 10-minute exercises, eBooks, audiobooks, and unique videos, all of which are intended to assist users in getting ready for their upcoming interactions with salespeople. Salespeople of all expertise levels can utilize the app because it is simple to use and navigate. Automobile Sales Success is a helpful tool for anyone wishing to succeed in the car sales sector because of its extensive resources and simple layout.

Available on the app store

Made in United States
Orlando, FL
11 April 2023

32002250R00157